The Moses
of
Wall Street

Investing The Right Way
For The Right Reasons

Praise for...

The Moses of Wall Street

I wish you wrote this book 15 years ago!

Thank you for writing such a simple yet powerful investing book. May God continue to bless you in all you do! I found it to be intensely insightful without a page of meaningless babble. You provided proof for your system and in doing so also offer hope and encouragement.

You presented an honest, credible book that explained how to make money using the markets. More importantly, you reveal the purpose and provider of money. While sharing sound financial principles that will last a life time your message of God's grace will last forever!

– **Cornel Rigby, MBA,** North Carolina

In my opinion, Ron Tank knows more about investing in the stock market than any investor I have ever met. More importantly, he teaches and shares that information with anyone who is willing to learn.

When Ron Tank speaks and teaches about God or investing, I listen very carefully. Because of his willingness to share his knowledge, my peers and I have received great dividends.

– **Lealand D. Dougherty,** Deputy Director Department of Defense (Retired) Information Technology Service Organization

Great book, well written, complex material made simple.

– **Amazon Reviewer**

Great Read. Very well written. A true story of redemption and God's abundance. Ron Tank shares his personal story of loss and reaching out to God for help.

Through his challenges Ron remained faithful and God allowed him to see a new way to invest in Wall Street. The outcome was significant financially and spiritually.

Now, through this book, Ron Tank shares the message God gave to him to show others a specific way to invest in the market that aligns with a principal God has shown throughout His Word.

– **Dean White, CA** (former Associate Pastor, Saddleback Church)

Ron Tank hit a home run with the publication of his book, "The Moses of Wall Street". He uses biblical principles to explain how to become successful in the stock market. This is a book I would highly recommend. His priorities are "rock-solid" along with his results.

– **Michael Thornton**

What a fascinating read — I was never really into 'playing' in the stock market, just wasn't my thing. It just seemed really complicated, cumbersome and a lot like gambling.

This book truly got me very interested and a bit excited on how I could possibly start to 'play' in the stock marketing with Ron's guidance.

Definitely pick this book up if you're interested in discovering how you can succeed in the stock market - thanks Ron!

– **Shannon M. Mccaffery, NJ**

After reading your book, I purchased your home study course and I took a look at GBP/JPY pair on a weekly chart and I think I see the triple tank in its uptrend. I have a buy trade going on now and I am up 304 pips.

– **Richard Wing,** Currency Trader, New York

This book will change the way you invest forever.

This book is powerful. Ron Tank's success alone has been inspiring. The stories are awe inspiring and you'll learn more about investing, than you knew before reading this book. Pick up a copy for you...and one for someone you truly care about.

– **Keith L., Vermont**

The Moses
of
Wall Street

Investing The Right Way
For The Right Reasons

by
Ron Tank

Trinity
PUBLISHING COMPANY

ISBN: 978-0-9907633-7-6

Cover Art and Design
Larry Barsky

Editing
Maura Leon

Proofreading
Melody Masi and Heather Taylor

Interior design
Rudy Milanovich

NOTICE: There is a risk in trading markets. Information contained herein is not and should not be construed as an offer, solicitation, or recommendation to buy or sell securities.

The information has been obtained from sources we believe to be reliable; however, no guarantee is made or implied with respect to its accuracy, timeliness, or completeness.

The information and content are subject to change without notice. The publisher and/or its individual officers, employees, or members of their families might, from time to time, have a position in the securities mentioned and may purchase or sell these securities in the future.

The publisher and/or its individual officers, employees, or members of their families might, from time to time, have financial interests with affiliates of companies whose securities have been discussed in this publication.

Dedication

This book is dedicated to my children, Ava and Wyatt.

Acknowledgments

Ava and Wyatt, *you are the reason for this book.* I hope and pray my obedience to God inspires you.

Sheryl, I thank you from the bottom of my heart for all of your support in life and in writing this book. I couldn't have done it without your encouragement, patience, and love.

Mom, you have been the perfect example, throughout my life, of God's unconditional love. You are truly my inspiration and my hero!

Dave, thank you for your support throughout our journey, and for being a terrific brother from the very beginning.

Thanks, from the bottom of my heart, to my late grandmother, Garnet Tank, who was my living example of biblical faith throughout her entire life.

Completing this book, the strategy guide, and the model book were the most challenging accomplishments of my life. They were only possible with God's direction, His patience with me, and the support of all of you.

To all of you: 1 Corinthians 13:13 says, "And now these three remain: faith, hope, and love. But the greatest of these is love," making the greatest three words I could ever say to you...

I LOVE YOU.

I want to especially thank David Boufford. Without your inspiration, encouragement, and support, it is possible this book would never have made it to print.

Also, my thanks go to William O'Neil, John Maxwell, Max Lucado, Jack Canfield, Zig Ziglar, Dr. Charles Stanley, Steve Harrison, Tim Paulson, and Adam Christing for making a direct impact upon my life and thereby contributing to this book. Thanks to Keith and Maura Leon at Babypie Publishing. With all that I am, I THANK YOU!

> *"If you would not be forgotten as soon as you are dead, either write something worth reading or do things worth writing."*
>
> ~*Benjamin Franklin*

Trinity Yard: Where Wall Street Ends and Church Begins

The cover is an artistic rendition of the current-day Trinity Church, sitting at the end of Wall Street. Founded in 1697 and later destroyed by the Great Fire of 1776, Trinity was rebuilt and remained in service until a severe snowstorm revealed structural issues in 1838. The second Trinity Church was torn down, rebuilt, and consecrated as the third Trinity Church on May 21, 1846. It remains there today.

If you would like to learn more about Trinity Church in New York, you can read the book, *Trinity: A Church, a Parish, a People*, by Dena Merriam.

Many thanks to Larry Barsky, the cover artist.

Contents

Where the Bible Meets Wall Street

"Ethics and spiritual principles should be the absolute basis of everything we do in life. All that we say. All that we think. In fact, if everything we did was structured from a foundation of ethics and spiritual principles, how could we not be successful?"

~Sir John Templeton

It's likely you have some experience with Wall Street. Maybe you're like me and make your own decisions concerning when to buy and sell stock. You may have a 401K, IRA, or some other retirement account involved with the stock market. Maybe your encounters with Wall Street are limited to what you hear on the news or have seen in a few of the popular Wall Street movies. Whatever your views, beliefs, or experiences are, I'm asking you to put them aside and let me share with you something very special I've discovered while spending nearly twenty years earning a living in the stock market.

My brother, Dave, and I sent our results in to *Investor's Business Daily* in response to an invitation in their paper. They wanted people to send in their investment results for the three-year period of 1998–2000. Several months later, we were profiled on the "Smart Investor" page, where they shared our story.

Dave had earned 1,820 percent, and I had posted a gain of 3,460 percent. (My gain was actually 5,000 percent because I had also withdrawn five hundred thousand dollars from my account during that time period.)

I know it's definitely not typical and sounds quite unreal. Had I not experienced it myself, I would have had a hard time believing it. But it is true. As you continue reading, be aware that you won't find much in this book that is typical. The subject matter is not typical. The results are not typical.

In 2014, I netted a gain of 1,124 percent in just seventeen days when $58,000 grew to over $700,000.

Bragging isn't my motivation, getting your attention is.

I've made my share of mistakes too, and I'll share them. But you deserve a good reason to give me a few valuable hours of your time. I honestly believe you'll be glad you did, and I greatly appreciate it.

I want your attention so I can share with you the most important discovery and tool I've encountered as a full-time investor over the past twenty years. You are about to see the basic method behind a system that will allow you to consistently do very well in the stock market.

Someone once told me that fewer than 10 percent of people who start reading a book ever finish it. Please take the time to read this entire book. Personally, I would suggest reading it three times. (You'll understand why later.) This book could be your doorway to a much brighter financial future.

I believe we live in the greatest country in the world.

Where better to invest our money than in the stock market of the United States?

Every year, there are thousands of entrepreneurs making something better or discovering a life-changing invention.

You have an opportunity to own a piece of some of the greatest businesses the earth has ever seen. They are here right now, and they just keep coming. Wall Street provides everyone the same amazing opportunity.

Whether you have a few thousand dollars and are new to investing or millions of dollars and decades of experience, you'll benefit tremendously and be surprised at how this book simplifies the stock market.

I've heard there are three things you should never discuss in public: God, money, and politics. I promise I won't talk about politics.

When I shared the beginnings of this book with a friend and pastor, his reply was, "Ron, it just sounds too good to be true."

I smiled and replied, "God's grace sounds too good to be true too, doesn't it?"

He smiled and agreed.

I'll show you why I know God wants you and me to be investors. You'll be surprised to learn exactly when you should start and what you must be willing to do to succeed. You'll discover what a great benefit it is to know that God is on your side.

You may have heard an expert or two on television telling you that timing the stock market in the short term can't be done. Even Warren Buffett admitted he can't, and he doesn't believe that anyone else can either. *But I say you can, and I'll show you how.*

I'll show you a secret that is hidden in plain sight, revealing your God-given *Decision-Maker DNA*. You'll be shocked to find that we have a common trait, and that it is the key to success when it comes to investing. It provides the foundation of *The Triple Tank*, which allows us to get into the stock market at just the right time, *eliminating risk and maximizing profits.*

There is one deadly sin you must avoid. You'll find it plastered all over the television. Likely, you haven't noticed the devastating power it has, until now, and I'll help you avoid it.

God wants you to be an investor, but as you begin to move forward and have success, you'll need to stay on the path of the good and faithful servant. I'll share the four deadly traps you must avoid and the three keys you must possess. They'll pave the road to continued success.

A great help to me are *The Ten Commandments of the Successful Investor*. They help me tremendously when it comes to preventing mistakes and keeping me close to God. I know they can do the same for you.

It's been said that the Bible talks more about money and personal finance than any other subject. Contrary to the popular myth that money is the root of all evil, the Bible actually tells us in 1 Timothy 6:10, "For the *love* of money is a root of all kinds of evil [emphasis added]." Loving money can lead to all sorts of bad things, but money itself is a wonderful tool. It can help build God's kingdom, provide for our families, and allow us to live fun and rewarding lives.

The goal of this book is not only to inspire and prosper you financially, but also to draw you nearer to God. I truly hope this book benefits you spiritually even more than financially. Being a successful investor is a good thing; being rich in God is even better.

After all, money is important, but it's not more important than God.

You're already on your way to investing the right way for the right reasons. Now, let's take a stroll down Wall Street. Come on, let's go!

Wall Street:
Investing or Gambling?

"I think there's a difference between a gamble and a calculated risk."

~Edmund H. North

11 Wall Street, New York, NY: home of the New York Stock Exchange

Wall Street has become synonymous with the financial markets of the United States. It is known as the premier financial capital of the world and is home to the headquarters of many of the world's most renowned financial businesses and market exchanges. Every weekday, tens of billions of dollars change hands through the exchange of stock in publicly traded companies.

It is an unimaginable feat.

What I find even more amazing is that anyone walking down Wall Street will discover that it dead-ends at the doors of Trinity Church. Trinity, founded in 1697, has been looking down Wall Street for a long, long time.

I suspect God intended for it to be that way.

Just a short walk from the New York Stock Exchange, you

could find yourself sitting inside Trinity, reading the Bible and learning more about Wall Street than you might ever imagine.

I would never have guessed, in a million years, that God's Word would hold a secret, hidden in plain sight, which would reveal a rock-solid foundation for investing.

But why wouldn't it?

The Bible is full of God's wisdom.

Why wouldn't it contain the key to success in our financial lives?

Did you know there are over eighteen hundred references to money and finances in the Bible?

Sometimes, I think we put the Bible in a box, believing it is only for our spiritual life.

The official beginnings of Wall Street came through the Buttonwood Agreement in 1792. The purpose was to provide more structure and reduce manipulation found in the trading auctions. The concerns people have today about Wall Street are not new.

What is the true purpose of the New York Stock Exchange?

To allow people to trade shares of companies they own — hopefully, for a profit.

The stock exchange provides an avenue for companies that have growth and financial soundness to offer for sale shares of the company to the public. A company raises money by selling shares of ownership — stock — to the public. The company can use the money in whatever manner it deems most appropriate for its continued growth. Those buying the shares now possess a piece of the company. The shares of stock are subject to increase or decrease in value over time. If a shareholder decides that the company's best days are behind it, they can sell their shares almost instantly. If they believe more good times are ahead, they can remain a shareholder and benefit from the appreciation of their stock as the company continues to grow and generate more shareholder value.

Wall Street isn't bad; it's just an address.

Unfortunately, a huge number of people believe that Wall Street is full of crime and rigged in favor of the money-hungry scoundrels who go there to find their next victim. We all remember Enron and Bernie Madoff, real examples of our worst fears.

Even movies about Wall Street promote ruthless ambition.

In the movie, *Wall Street,* Gordon Gecko says, "The point is, Ladies and Gentlemen, that greed, for lack of a better word, is good."

Say what, Gordon?

Didn't the Enron crew and Bernie all go to prison?

What could be worse than losing your hard-earned money, except for maybe ending up in jail?

Whatever you do, don't let a few bad apples scare you away from one of the greatest opportunities available, an opportunity in which you can own a piece of the pie and benefit from America's success.

What's good about Wall Street?

One of every two start-up businesses fails in its first five years. Seven out of ten fail within ten years. Depending on the source, survival rate statistics can be much worse. Those businesses remaining may not be tremendously profitable. With a little effort, the stock market allows you to discover and own those companies that have defeated the odds and built very profitable businesses. You and I can profit without building a business of our own.

It provides a means for the average American to own part of a successful company and generate a profit through the appreciation of the stock they own. What a huge opportunity for those who save some money and are willing to invest it! Opportunities come about all the time. It's just a matter of whether you'll be there, looking to see the next huge winner, like McDonald's, Microsoft, Dell Computer, Yahoo, Cisco Systems, Google, and so on.

Wall Street is a place where hard work pays off and creates wealth for those who understand it and get involved. Look at Warren Buffett and Sir John Templeton, two greats on the noble side who have helped others tremendously.

It's easy to believe that Wall Street is a place for gamblers.

Let's imagine you're at a horse race. The track lets you place a bet on a horse. Let's say the race is three laps. You watch intently as the race begins.

Ding, ding, ding — off they go!

Now imagine that as they finish the first lap, your horse is in first place. But halfway into lap two, your horse slips back into fourth place.

Oh, no!

As he enters lap three, your horse is in deeper trouble and is now in eighth place. It is not looking good at all.

I think I'll go back and reduce my bet.

Sorry! You can't do that.

What?

You mean I'm stuck?

I can't lessen the damage if my horse loses?

Sorry! You're in it to win it, as they say. You'll just have to sit and watch. That's gambling.

Gambling asks you to give your money and hope — without a reasonable chance of winning and with absolutely no way of limiting your loss. You really own nothing, and most times, you'll end up with nothing.

What a lousy position to be in!

If, on the other hand, you are investing and you buy stock in a company that trades on the stock exchange, many options are available to you.

For example, let's say you buy shares in McDonald's. If, over the next few weeks or months, McDonald's stock goes down, and you begin to lose money, you have the option of selling some or all of your stock, limiting your loss by taking decisive action. Another great advantage to investing is that you can also buy more stock if it is going up in value and working well.

These adjustments are available to an investor.

This sounds like such a basic skill, *but all too many investors do this backwards or not at all.*

If you put your money in the stock market and then do nothing but hope that in ten, twenty, or thirty years it will be worth more, what does that sound more like — investing or gambling?

Being an owner of stock also requires you to be a manager. You must understand that owning the right stock at the wrong time can cost you money. You must learn to be on guard for many harmful characteristics that can derail you — things such as greed, pride, and fear, any and all of which can bring defeat to most investors.

Managing ownership of stock requires you to manage both the

stock and yourself. Fortunately, the Bible has many answers on how to understand and handle ourselves.

It speaks to the value of being generous, not greedy; humble, not prideful; and bold, not timid.

God's Word has many principles that teach us how to avoid the characteristics which will cause us not only harm in the stock market but also grief in our everyday life. We can learn proper management techniques to address ourselves and our investments. Management requires us to make decisions and adjust as we gather new information over time.

We must manage.

That's what is terrific about the stock market. You can own any publicly traded company you want to in a matter of seconds. If you choose to, and you should, you can manage that ownership, over time, using sound rules and guidelines. You have the opportunity to generate profits according to your abilities. When you buy stock, you own an asset and can manage it. You can be a steward.

Being a hopeful steward is good, but being a good steward requires more than hope as a primary strategy.

You must have a system with rules to guide you and keep you out of harm's way. God gave us the Ten Commandments through Moses so that we could live a successful life. I believe He has called me to share with you my system and the investing commandments that guide me in being a good steward. You'll find *The Ten Commandments of the Successful Investor* near the end of the book.

God Wants You to Be an Investor

"My concern is not whether God is on our side; my greatest concern is to be on God's side, for God is always right."

~Abraham Lincoln

Here's how I know that God wants you and me to be investors:

In the book of Matthew, the parable of the talents demands that we do well with the money God has entrusted to us, regardless of how much money we have or how fearful we may be. The parable involves three servants and the handling of the money that the master had entrusted to them. At times, I've heard something like "abilities" substituted for "money" when this parable is taught.

I'm going to zero in on exactly what is taking place and share with you what I believe is the main message.

Let's read it first as printed in the 1984 New International Version:

Matthew 25:14–30

¹⁴ Again, it will be like a man going on a journey, who called his servants and entrusted his property to them. ¹⁵ To one he gave five talents of money, to another two talents, and to another one talent, each according to his ability. Then he went on his journey. ¹⁶ *The man who had received the five talents went at once and put his money to work and gained five more.* ¹⁷ *So also, the one with the two talents gained two more.* ¹⁸ *But the man who had received the one talent went off, dug a hole in the ground and hid his master's money.*

¹⁹ *After a long time the master of those servants returned and settled accounts with them.* ²⁰ *The man who had received the five talents brought the other five. "Master," he said, "you entrusted me with five talents. See, I have gained five more."*

²¹ *His master replied, "Well done, good and faithful servant! You have been faithful with a few things; I will put you in charge of many things. Come and share your master's happiness!"*

²² *The man with the two talents also came. "Master," he said, "you entrusted me with two talents; see, I have gained two more."*

²³ *His master replied, "Well done, good and faithful servant! You have been faithful with a few things; I will put you in charge of many things. Come and share your master's happiness!"*

²⁴ *Then the man who had received the one talent came. "Master," he said, "I knew that you are a hard man, harvesting where you have not sown and gathering where you have not scattered seed.* ²⁵ *So I was afraid and went out and hid your talent in the ground. See, here is what belongs to you."*

²⁶ *His master replied, "You wicked, lazy servant! So you knew that I harvest where I have not sown and gather where I have not scattered seed?* ²⁷ *Well then, you should have put my money on deposit with the bankers, so that when I returned I would have received it back with interest.*

²⁸ *"Take the talent from him and give it to the one who has the ten talents.* ²⁹ *For everyone who has will be given more, and he will have an abundance. Whoever does not have, even what he has will be taken from him.* ³⁰ *And throw that worthless servant outside, into the darkness, where there will be weeping and gnashing of teeth."*

LESSONS FROM THE PARABLE

Lesson One: To have more, we must increase our abilities.

Each servant was given to according to his ability (verse 15).

If we want to have more to manage, we must first demonstrate the ability to handle what we are entrusted with right now.

Where should we go in order to find the wisdom needed to increase our abilities?

"But remember the Lord your God, for it is he who gives you the ability to produce wealth, and so confirms his covenant, which he swore to your ancestors, as it is today." — Deuteronomy 8:18

It is God that gives us the *abilities* we need.

Lesson Two: We need to start right now.

When should we start investing, or at least, seeking out opportunities?

At once!

Verse 16 makes it clear.

The servant set out when?

At once.

He took the directive he had received and implemented it right away.

He was to gain more with that which had been entrusted to him.

Lesson Three: We are to be investors.

There are two reasons why this is true:

1. Because we know that each of the first two servants doubled their money. Let me repeat that. *Each of the first*

two servants doubled their money. This requires some skill and effort. We know it doesn't happen by accident.

2. The last servant buried his money and returned only what he was given. He was reprimanded and told, "you should have put my money on deposit with the bankers, so that when I returned I would have received it back with interest." In other words, if you weren't willing to invest and make something substantial out of it, then you should have at least done the very minimum and earned interest.

Are you so afraid of losing what you have that you are considering burying it in your back yard?

What brings this to life even more is to consider what a talent is equal to today.

In his book, *The Cure for the Common Life*, Max Lucado says, "Before 'talent' meant skill, it meant money. It represented the largest unit of accounting in the Greek currency—10,000 denarii. According to the parable of the workers, a denarius represented a day's fair wages (Matthew 20:2)."

A talent equals 10,000 denarii and a denarius equals a day's fair wages.

What is a fair day's wages in today's money?

According to the US Census Bureau, the median income for someone in the United States in 2008–09 was $49,945. If you worked 40 hours per week for 50 weeks, you would have worked 2000 hours in a year, and $49,945 divided by 2000 equals $24.97 per hour. The average day's pay would be $24.97 times 8 hours, which equals $199.76.

The current value of a denarius equals $199.76. A talent is worth 10,000 times $199.76, which equals $1,997,600.

A talent is worth $1,997,600 in today's money.

Let's round that to a talent being worth almost two million dollars. So the servants were given the equivalent of two, four, and ten million dollars.

If someone handed that amount of money to you with the responsibility of doing more than handing it over to a banker, could you double it, or would you hide it?

Each servant was offered feedback on the job they did. The first two were commended and put in charge of more things. They were good stewards, or managers, of that which was entrusted to them. They were also invited to share in their master's happiness.

What a great example!

We are to be *in charge of* instead of owning.

We need to do better than just giving it to a banker. Besides, nowadays, you almost have to pay a banker to keep your money.

How bad is that?

We need to invest wisely, and then it might also be said of us, "Well done, good and faithful servant!" We can share in the owner's happiness.

In Psalm 24:1, God tells us, "The earth is the Lord's, and everything in it, the world, and all who live in it..."

What is ours?

Nothing.

What is ours to manage?

Everything God entrusts to us. The third servant got it all

wrong. He was so afraid of his master that he couldn't envision doing anything but hiding the money, so he could give it back.

What was his feedback from the master?

The master scorned him for not having the common sense to at least give it to a banker to earn interest. His talent was taken from him and given to the one who had ten talents, and he was thrown into the darkness.

Although giving our money to a banker who will pay us interest is better than hiding it, God wants us—expects us—to invest what He has entrusted to us.

Wealth and happiness are the by-products of a job well done.

According to Matthew 25:29, we gain more or keep none.

THE INVESTOR MINDSET AUDIO PROGRAM

What's inside the successful investor's mind? In this audio, I'll share how I believe a successful investor must think. Plus, you'll discover how my faith and lessons I've learned from the Bible provide a rock-solid mindset for investing in the stock market. This audio was originally created just for my coaching program and is the first topic I share with my clients.

As part of the FREE Book Bonus, you can download the Investor Mindset Audio by visiting: www.RonTank.com/BookBonus

The Darkest Hour

"It is during our darkest moments that we must focus to see the light."

~Aristotle Onassis

Depending on your age, you might remember the Stock Market Crash of 1929 and the Great Depression that followed. Or maybe you had a parent or grandparent who told you about it. I'm glad my exposure was limited to just reading about it.

I've been around long enough to witness the October crash of 1987, when the NASDAQ Composite lost 36 percent in just seventeen days. I was in college at the time, and it really had no effect on me, but it sure did make a big splash in the news.

Then in 1998, the market tanked on fears of foreign markets crashing, and the spill-over could take down certain hedge funds in the United States. The NASDAQ was pummeled 32 percent in less than three months.

For our generation, the markets always came back rather quickly. The days of depression, like those in the early 1930s, were a thing of the past.

Right?

Wrong!

The year 2000 ushered in a similar implosion which almost

mirrored that of the three-year bear market of 1929–1932. The NASDAQ Composite declined 78 percent from 2000–2002.

Talk about dark!

As if that wasn't bad enough, in October of 2007, the NASDAQ once again peaked and would decline 55 percent over the next sixteen months before the damage finally ended in March, 2009.

We've seen so-called blue-chip stocks like Lehman Brothers and General Motors go bankrupt. You may remember the Enron disaster or maybe Bernie Madoff and his Ponzi scheme. You've probably seen movies, like *Wall Street*, in which Gordon says that greed is good, or the more recent movie, *The Wolf of Wall Street*, which appears to glorify debauchery, fraud, and manipulation.

I'm not surprised when I hear people say things like:

"The market is rigged."

"The stock market is just one big Ponzi scheme."

Some have said:

"The little guy just can't win."

"Nowadays, you need insider information to beat the market."

In 2013, Gallup reported that only 52 percent of Americans had money invested in stocks, which was the lowest percentage since 1998. Over the past fifteen years, our government and the Federal Reserve have pulled out every tool in their tool box to get our economy and the financial markets back on solid footing.

If you owned a mutual fund or had a retirement account invested in the stock market on January 1, 2000, then ten years later, on December 31, 2009, it is very likely you lost money. If your mutual fund or retirement account performed similar to the NASDAQ, you may have lost 40 percent or more. The NASDAQ was down 44.2 percent over that ten-year period. You may have fared a little better than that, or you may not have.

When we put our money to work for us in the market, we should expect it to work for us and earn a profit.

I wouldn't work for an employer for ten years expecting him to pay me but, instead, paying him. If I wouldn't do this, *why would I let my money do that very thing?*

If buy and hold were gold, professional investment advisors would be dinosaurs — a thing of the past.

After all, why pay a professional if his best advice is always to stay the course?

Have you been involved with the stock market over the past five, ten, or even twenty years?

If so, have you, at times, found yourself hiding in a foxhole, trying to avoid the financial warfare?

Good news! You are about to receive a big dose of psychological sunshine.

If you are just getting started, then you are in a great position. You will not be burdened with past experience. You may have opinions and ideas, and that's all right. I would be surprised if you didn't. Don't let them get in your way right now.

Whether you have no experience or a lot, I suggest you imagine a trash can sitting beside you, toss all those opinions in the can, and leave them there as you consider something new. It will be a good exercise that will serve you well throughout your life.

Often, when the stock market is in trouble, you may hear older gentlemen on financial television programs referring to a process through which the markets are going. There is often talk about processes in general, but no one ever gives you a good explanation as to what the process is. This makes for good sound bites, but it is not much help when the market is tanking hard.

I really don't know whether the process they are referring to is the same as the one I'll show you here. If it's not, then maybe I can be of help to them as well.

You are about to discover something that the vast majority of professional investors do not know.

Two great investors, Warren Buffett and the late Sir John Templeton, both understood the importance of interpreting greed and fear.

Warren Buffett once said, "We simply attempt to be fearful when others are greedy and to be greedy only when others are fearful."

Great! But how, exactly, do you do that?

Sir John Templeton said, "To buy when others are despondently selling and to sell when others are avidly buying requires the greatest fortitude and pays the greatest reward."

He also said, "It is extremely difficult to go against the crowd — to buy when everyone else is selling or has sold, to buy when things look darkest, to buy when so many experts are telling you that stocks in general, or in this particular industry, or even in this particular company, are risky right now."

How might you know when it is the darkest or when most everyone is fearful?

If you were outside in the middle of nowhere at midnight with no moon, it would be the darkest.

Or at least, it would be close, right?

But when it comes to the financial markets, someone always seems to think the sky hasn't fallen yet. And then there are those who think the sky has already fallen.

So how would you really know if the darkest hour is behind you?

The good news is that you don't need to know when it is the darkest. You only need to know when people *think* it is the darkest and take action to get out of the dark.

In the stock market, when the last of the potential sellers have sold, it is the darkest.

Wouldn't you agree?

How do you know when the last holdouts have sold?

In the game of baseball, it takes three strikes to send the batter to the dugout or three outs before you switch sides. In the investment arena, it often takes three declines to convince investors to switch sides. If you are like most investors, it's very likely you have been switching sides at the wrong time.

You can learn to identify the points in time when the stock market almost always bottoms, the darkest hour, and how you can use this information to profit, regardless of what the news media and the so-called professionals are saying.

Could Warren Buffett Be Wrong?

"Within the covers of the Bible are the answers for all problems men face, if we'd only look there."

~Ronald Reagan

In the book, *The Warren Buffett Way*, by Robert G. Hagstrom, we read, "Over the long term, common stock prices have a remarkable relationship to the underlying economic value of the business, he said. As a company's economic value increases over time, so too will the price of the shares of the business. If on the other hand, the company falters, the stock price will reflect this. Of course, over shorter periods, Buffet learned that the price of stocks will move above or below its business value, *dependent more on emotions than economics* [emphasis added]."

What if we could identify a company with good long-term underlying economic value at a time when the stock price is down due to emotions in the short term?

I'm going to introduce you to a method that will allow you to get into the stock market at just the right time, based on the way you are programmed to make decisions. The foundation of the system is the *Decision-Maker DNA*, a biblical secret hidden in plain sight. The *Decision-Maker DNA* reveals itself as *The Triple Tank* in the stock market.

You'll discover how *The Triple Tank* creates the perfect timing, allowing you to annihilate risk and put momentum on your side. The *Decision-Maker DNA* and *The Triple Tank will allow you to do what the experts, even Warren Buffett, claim is impossible.*

What do they claim is impossible?

In *The Warren Buffett Way*, we're also told, "**Buffet cannot predict short-term market movements and does not believe that anyone else can** [emphasis added]."

But when it comes to market movements, could Warren Buffett be wrong?

Don't misunderstand me, I love Warren Buffett. He has been able to do what few others have, which is to buy great companies, manage them well, and remain unruffled through turbulent times, making his shareholders very happy. I do, however, believe he is wrong — at least, concerning one's ability to predict market movements in the short term. I'd love to sit down and show him how I do it using *The Triple Tank*. He might be surprised by how it uncovers the point in time when people are the most fearful, providing impeccable timing for entering a position in the stock market.

THE AHA MOMENT

It was 2006. I had been involved in a men's weekly Bible study group at our church for about eleven years. Our small group of eight or ten met on Thursday evenings.

One evening, I sat down in our living room with Bible and lesson book in hand. My plan was to prepare for the upcoming meeting.

The television was on, and instead of turning it off, I turned it to one of my favorite places, The Discovery Channel. There was a great show on about an unarmed man who would approach wild lions in Africa. His goal was to get the lions to accept his presence and to see how close to them he could get.

At first, it seemed almost suicidal, and as you can imagine, it caught my attention.

I opened my Bible and began to read in Acts, chapter 10.

Not long after I began reading, the show interrupted me and really grabbed my attention. They described how a lion would warn an approaching intruder. The lion would even tolerate a second approach but would use a more alarming warning signal. Then, they described how the lion would deny a man a third attempt at approaching him. If you didn't heed his first and second warnings and approached him a third time, you were his dinner!

As I continued reading my Bible, it described Peter seeing a vision. A voice told him what to do, and after Peter incorrectly interpreted the meaning, the voice spoke to him a second time.

Then I read in verse 16, "This happened three times, and immediately the sheet was taken back to heaven."

At that very moment, I could see a picture in my head of the NASDAQ Composite Index in the fall of 2005. I could clearly see three distinct declines, followed by a big advance in the NASDAQ over the next several months.

Could it be?

Were the market, a lion, and Peter all acting upon a third occurrence?

Yes!

Goose bumps peppered me, leaving me with chills. I couldn't believe it.

Did God just open a window and let me see what I wouldn't have otherwise seen?

Yes! Yes! Yes!

It would later become known as the *Decision-Maker DNA*, a trait God clearly built into each one of us, the animals, and the world around us. Because people make up the activity in the stock market, we'll even see it there.

This insight has become the foundation of my *Triple Tank System*.

Investing money in the stock market involves psychology and, most often, predictable behavior. We'll study this in depth and learn how the number three is unlike any other. Its ability to induce predictable behavior has been demonstrated repeatedly throughout history.

William J. O'Neil, who has been investing since the 1950s, is one of the most brilliant stock market investors of our time. He wrote two great books, *How to Make Money in Stocks* and *The Successful Investor*, both of which I highly recommend you **study**. But the book I wish he had written twenty years ago would have focused on what Mr. O'Neil commented on in *How to Make Money in Stocks*.

He said, "Bear markets normally show three legs of price movement down."

I suspect that this sentence is the most unexplained, overlooked, and undervalued statement in his book.

He also said, "History can repeat itself. If you have solid information about how markets behaved during certain past incidents, then you can develop better judgment for the future."

I would also expand William O'Neil's statement concerning three legs down to include them occurring in shorter-term intermediate market corrections and individual stocks, not just bear markets. In the next several chapters, you'll see the value in understanding three legs down, which I'll refer to as *The Triple Tank*. We'll also examine history, so we can be better prepared for the future.

I've noticed that the same thing can happen when reading the Bible. Often, we read verses but never really stop to examine their significance.

Do we fully understand what they mean?

If not, do we take the time to more fully understand?

I know I'm guilty of not asking myself the relevance of three legs down when reading O'Neil's book. It is only briefly mentioned and not explained.

Because of God's intervention in the aha moment and a lot of homework since, you're going to get a full explanation of what it means and how relevant it is — something I wish I had known twenty years ago.

In today's world, people seem to either ignore the Bible or expect it to be found only in church on Sunday. It seems like the phrase, "separation of church and state," has been interpreted to mean, "Read the Bible if you want to, but keep it at home."

What a shame.

D.L. Moody once said, "One thing I have noticed in studying the Word of God, and that is, when a man is filled with the Spirit he deals largely with the Word of God, whereas the man who is filled with his own ideas refers rarely to the Word of God. He gets along without it, and you seldom see it mentioned in his discourses."

The amazing thing is that, when you bring the Bible into your career, you may see things totally differently. Your eyes may focus and observe the detail in the world around you in a different light—a good light that reveals a truth your eyes had not seen before.

Zig Ziglar, in his book, *God's Way Is Still the Best Way*, said it so well:

> "More and more Christians are taking God into the corporate offices, board rooms, and break rooms where they work."

> …

> "To be a good employee you must obey the Ten Commandments. You've got to be a hard worker. You've got to be dependable, honest, sincere, committed to the company's well-being, give it your best shot at all times, be kind to your fellow employees, and just in general employ character qualities that are good—qualities that just happen to come directly out of the Bible!"

> …

> "I have learned from many of these people that doing things God's way leads to better business practices and that His greatest blessings are, as I like to say, the things that money can't buy!"

Well said, Zig!

If you haven't read his book, please do so. It is terrific.

If we would more often let God into all areas of our lives, what a dramatic change we might see in the world around us! The Bible has far more to offer than one might expect.

Your Decision-Maker DNA™

"You can't reach success in investment if you don't think independently."

~Warren Buffett

There is really nothing new occurring in the stock market.

King Solomon said, "What has been will be again, what has been done will be done again; there is nothing new under the sun. Is there anything of which one can say, 'Look! This is something new'? It was here already, long ago; it was here before our time." (Ecclesiastes 1:9–10)

Sometimes, we do discover something new even though it has been there before our time.

After all, the earth has always been round, but we didn't always know it. It was new to us in AD 200, when Galileo proved the earth was spherical even though it had been round long before AD 200.

I've been investing professionally for almost twenty years. During this time, God opened a window that allowed me to see something new—a timeless secret hidden in plain sight in God's Word. It is the foundation of an identifiable, repeating event—occurring in the financial markets—that can be used to eliminate risk and maximize profits. The origins can be directly linked to the Bible.

In Genesis, chapter 1 tells us that God created everything in six days, including human beings. When God made us, He included a wonderful trait in our DNA. While other aspects of our DNA identify our uniqueness, there is a *common* trait built into all creatures, even animals. It has been passed on to everyone since Adam and Eve. We'll call it the *Decision-Maker DNA*.

In the last hundred-plus years, the stock market has become a tremendous opportunity, providing a way to invest in the businesses of this country and those around the world. The stock market has many aspects that affect its movement every day, but none of them are more relevant than human nature.

The stock market is human nature on display.

What is human nature?

By nature, we tend to be greedy, prideful, fearful, and hopeful — especially when it comes to money.

So until the financial markets no longer involve human beings and their emotions, the *Decision-Maker DNA* will make waves and continue indefinitely.

What is the *Decision-Maker DNA*?

It is a key trait you frequently use to understand, accept, or believe. *The Triple Tank* is a direct result of the *Decision-Maker DNA*. The *Decision-Maker DNA* explains how and why *The Triple Tank* signals rock bottom in a stock or market index almost every time you find it.

People haven't changed since God created man long ago. We think just like the people of biblical times.

Once you understand this and believe it, you'll have an uncommon advantage in the financial markets that you can use time and time again.

How hard is *The Triple Tank* to find?

It is as simple as counting to three.

No kidding!

But human nature and all the scary news will make it harder than you think when it comes time to use your newly found advantage. Right now, there are thousands—maybe even millions—of investors listening to scary news on television every year and selling at exactly the wrong time. Just correcting this one mistake could have a huge impact on your financial house.

LIONS AND BULLS AND BEARS, OH MY!

The story that follows is a result of thinking about my aha moment and then doing some homework over the next several years. It will fully explain the *Decision-Maker DNA* and *The Triple Tank*. If your television is on, you may want to turn it off because this one will keep you thinking and require your full attention.

Be careful…lions are roaming about!

Deep in the African bush, a four-hundred-pound male lion is at the top of the food chain. He understands his environment and knows how to survive. Nature may inflict pain upon him through lack of food or water, but it is man who can destroy him. If man makes a mistake and doesn't understand the language of the lion, he can quickly become a mere memory of the African bush and its king.

A lion in the African bush will often react to an approaching man in a predictable manner. Upon being approached, he graciously provides you with two warnings. The third time, you become the equivalent of a butcher's prime T-bone steak!

When it comes to being threatened, our actions, just like the lion's, can be predictable.

You must realize that psychology induces behavior. If you can understand this today, then you can use it to your advantage tomorrow.

Learning how psychology works is paramount if you want to become a good steward of your money in the stock market. By applying the principles contained here, you will have a deeper understanding of the number three and how it can profit you and save you thousands in the future. You'll be willing to sell investments before big trouble begins, and you'll be back in the stock market before the vast majority of people realize the carnage is over and it's safe to be invested again. The psychological damage experienced by many in between these two points in time will have passed you by. You will be in the minority, but it will be a very relaxed, confident, and secure minority.

Let's go for a walk in the jungle for a lesson in lion behavior.

1. When posed with a threat, a lion rarely reacts to anything the first time. In order to evade a possible confrontation which could lead to injury, he is willing to warn an approaching man who invades his space. If you get too close, the lion will flip his tail in a very intentional and purposeful way. This is his warning to you for invading his domain. It demonstrates his discomfort.

    If you respect this warning by backing away, he will remain still, resting, most likely, under a shady tree in the bush, content that you have acknowledged his warning.

2. After some time, you may approach this lion again, and he will allow you to get somewhat closer on the second attempt. Shortly after clearly passing your previous stopping point, you will encounter another warning.

This warning will make your hair stand up on end. The lion will unleash a blood-curdling roar and may lunge in your direction.

If you are quick to reward the lion by once again backing away, you will likely be spared. But you have managed to anger the lion. The first encroachment only brought a flip of the tail and got his attention. The second approach made him angry, and he definitely made you aware of it.

3. Now, we come to the part that involves the participation of your life insurance agent. If you decide to approach this lion a third time, you will not be given a warning. Upon going beyond the point where you stopped previously, you will become the T-bone of the day!

Now, you'll need to switch roles and think a little differently. Pretend that you are the lion and the man represents the stock market.

1. After the market has sustained many days of institutional selling, the major market index will break down and drop rather hard and quickly. This initial drop is the beginning of what we will refer to as **Leg 1**. You have been encroached upon by the market, and it likely has your attention. You've probably made a note of it, but your confidence still abounds. As with the man approaching the lion, the market will also acknowledge your irritation. The selling will subside, and a rally will begin.

   This is equivalent to the man backing away from the lion. Most investors will feel good again, unaware of the impending danger.

2. After a short period of time, the market will begin its descent into **Leg 2**, and just like the man approaching the lion, it will continue beyond the first stopping point.

As it does, you will likely respond as the lion did — with anger but with no action. How dare the market encroach on you more than it did the first time!

Again, the market will back away, rewarding you for sitting tight and not selling. The difference between the man approaching the lion and the market approaching you begins now. The market has a desire to see if you will T-bone it!

3. After the second drop and the passing of some time, the market will come at you a third time, and as it does, you will be angered quickly. You will not move until you see that it has gone past its second stopping point. You doubt that it will do so, but when it does, your trust has been violated, and you take action now. You are furious!

    What is the action you take?

    The lion would eat the man. You simply sell whatever you own at the time.

    The third drop will bring an end to the downward slide in the market.

    Why does it end here?

    Your *Decision-Maker DNA* has convinced you to take action. By this point in time, anyone willing to sell has done so. If you didn't sell by now, you likely never would for any reason.

Nothing helps you to understand more than seeing something in action. The next several pages will show you the *Decision-Maker DNA* in action — both in the stock market and in the Bible.

I'm going to follow the advice of Winston Churchill who said, "If you have an important point to make, don't try to be subtle or clever. Use a pile driver. Hit the point once. Then come back and hit it again. Then hit it a third time — a tremendous whack."

The NASDAQ Composite in 2004: *The Triple Tank* — Part I

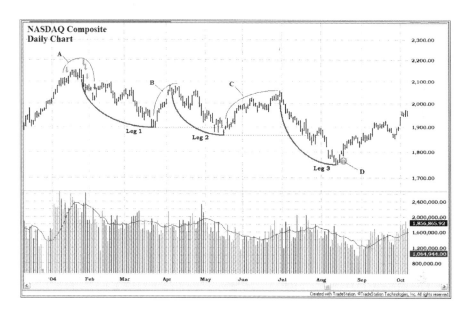

1. Institutional selling is detected at **POINT A**. This begins the process and is the start of the ensuing correction or bear market. From here, the NASDAQ suffers a 19-percent loss, in total, that lasts approximately seven months. **Leg 1** illustrates the first time the market gets your attention after the damage was inflicted at **POINT A**. This endures for approximately two months.

    The first drop is equivalent to the man approaching the lion for the first time. At the bottom of this leg is where the lion would be purposefully flipping his tail in disapproval, after which the man would back away. As you can see here at **POINT B**, the markets will respect your concern and also rally back, bringing a little hope and trust your way.

2. In a short period of time, the market will begin falling a second time. This time, you may be like the lion and really not expect the market to pass by the spot where it first stopped. But the market will pass the low point set by **Leg 1** and continue to pressure you with **Leg 2**.

   Like the lion, you'll be angry by now. The lion would be growling and threatening toward the man. The man would acknowledge this threat and reward the lion for warning him by backing away once again. The market will do likewise and rally back again at **POINT C**.

3. Now, the game would be up for the man if he desired to live. For the unsuspecting investor, the painful end is elusive. **Leg 3** is often the fastest and most severe. At about the time the lion would be running full speed to get his T-bone, which would be somewhere after the bottom of **Leg 2** has been passed and before the end of **Leg 3**, anger and fear will be quick to bring action on your part. If you are ever going to sell, you will now.

You may be thinking: *This doesn't happen to me because I don't look at charts.*

But it *is* happening to you because you *feel* the very thing that is taking place in the NASDAQ chart above.

You may not see it, but you will feel it.

Unfortunately for anyone ending up here, the damage has been done. Due to the psychological damage, the start of the next bull market will be next to impossible to recognize. The battle has taken its toll, and most investors will give up after such a harrowing experience.

Unfortunately for the victim, the beginning of the next bull market is the most crucial time to be positive and ready to get involved. In this case, the next bull market starts at **POINT D**. From this point, the NASDAQ races up 20 percent in just over five months.

Can you see how your psychology can become an enemy, keeping you from being objective at the very bottom, which is exactly when you need to be positive and patiently waiting for the new bull market to start?

A better understanding and preparedness will equip you for success.

You must avoid the psychological warfare. If you are aware of the process, you should be able to make big profits by selling when the institutions are also selling and sparing yourself the train wreck in psychology. There is a BONUS: You'll save thousands by staying out during the correction or bear market, whichever it may be.

During the third leg down, you should be sitting tight and watching for the rally that will start the new bull market. This rally will come. As most investors are throwing everything out the window, you will be watching the strong stocks and the market for the sign to be involved once again. Other investors will be psychologically damaged and unprepared for the next bull move to begin. And begin it will.

A huge strategic advantage is gained by understanding how market corrections and bear markets present themselves. You can avoid being a hostage. Three is the key that unlocks the treasure chest of understanding. It's inherent in the lion not to trust a man three times. A similar case can be made for a man and his reaction to the stock market. For this reason, it is critical for us to recognize the *Decision-Maker DNA*, a trait that has existed far longer than the market itself.

Does every correction or bear market appear as a *Triple Tank*?

No.

But *The Triple Tank* is a golden nugget every time you find it. And what's even better: The failure rate is almost zero.

Is there a time when you are almost guaranteed a profit in the stock market?

Yes!

Directly after a *Triple Tank* has occurred.

PETER'S VISION

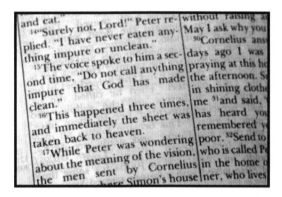

In Acts, chapter 10, Peter struggles with a vision. Verse 11 tells us that Peter sees what appears to be a large sheet, let down from heaven, containing all kinds of animals. The Lord speaks to him with instructions, but Peter fails to understand. The Lord speaks to him once again, but he still does not understand. Verse 16 tells us this happens three times. Peter finally comes to understand the vision that would change the world and reports it in verses 34–36:

> [34]*Then Peter began to speak: "I now realize that God does not show favoritism* [35]*but accepts men from every nation who fear him and do what is right.* [36]*This is the message God sent to the people of Israel, telling the good news of peace through Jesus Christ, who is Lord of all."*

Just like Peter, when information or an event isn't clear or we don't fully understand, we'll need to experience it three times before we understand, accept, or believe.

If the *Decision-Maker DNA* appears to be somewhat obscure to you at this point, that is perfectly understandable. One story about a lion really doesn't make for much proof.

But do you want to attempt to prove the lion story wrong?

If you're willing to volunteer an attempt, let me know — because I am definitely not!

The stock market and the Bible may exhibit the *Decision-Maker DNA* one time, but does it occur enough to prove it as a real trait that is common to all?

In other words, is it something you can count on and actually use?

I considered the same question, many times, when God first revealed the principle to me. I'd like to continue to show you the truth that was revealed to me.

It just keeps getting more and more real.

The NASDAQ Composite in the Fall of 2005: *The Triple Tank* — Part II

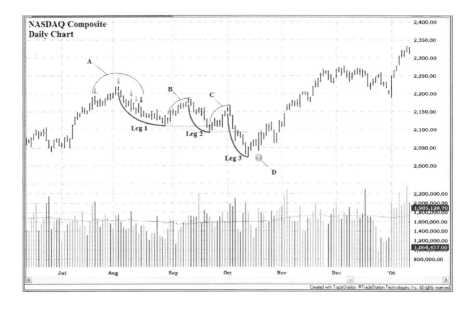

Briefly, let's set the stage and see how it works again.

- You're enjoying a healthy market and hoping it continues upwards.

- You encounter trouble during **POINT A**, and **Leg 1** occurs.

- **POINT B**, the first rally, builds a little hope. Watch out for greed.

- You are likely feeling better and hoping this won't happen again, but then, **Leg 2** occurs.

- When it does, you become angry, but then, **POINT C** comes along and creates some hope once again.

- You are somewhat suspicious, but you are paying full attention to the situation.

- Now, **Leg 3** occurs, and you reluctantly admit that the market just isn't working.

- After three doses of losing money, you identify the repetitiveness, and your fear of losing more prompts you to throw in the towel.

Game over!

Please take note of this very important point because it's worth a thousand times the value of the time it's taking you to read this book:

You should be buying, not selling, in leg three of *The Triple Tank.*

Unless you understand the *Decision-Maker DNA*, you'll likely sell out at exactly the wrong time. You'll be left behind when the bottom comes, and very likely, you'll freeze up and have a hard time getting back in. Over time, this can be devastating. You'll get frustrated during the rally and, finally, tell yourself that everything is okay. Likely, you'll buy in too late—just as institutional selling stops the market.

You may be asking yourself: *Couldn't I buy into the stock market and just stay in?*

While most of the expert financial advisors make the claim that you should just get in and stay in because, over time, the stock market provides the best returns, **I've always wondered why so much training is required by all of those financial experts, only to have their best advice be to stay in.**

For that method of investing, it doesn't appear that any training or skill is required at all, does it?

It is apparent to me that the past decade or more is proving the need for a better strategy.

PAUL'S THORN

The Thorn in the Flesh

⁷And lest I should be exalted above measure by the abundance of the revelations, a thorn in the flesh was given to me, a messenger of Satan to buffet me, lest I be exalted above measure. ⁸Concerning this thing I pleaded with the Lord three times that it might depart from me. ⁹And He said to me, "My grace is sufficient for you, for My strength is made perfect in weakness." Therefore most gladly I will rather boast in my infirmities, that the power of Christ may rest ... take pleasure in infirmities, in

In 2 Corinthians 12, Paul contends with a thorn in the flesh. In verse 7, he tells us the thorn was a messenger of Satan to torment him.

Paul goes on in verses 8 and 9, saying, "Three times I pleaded with the Lord to take it away from me. But He said to me, 'My grace is sufficient for you, for my power is made perfect in weakness.' Therefore I will boast all the more gladly about my weaknesses, so that Christ's power may rest on me."

We see here that Paul asked God to remove a thorn from his flesh three times. After three times, he stopped asking and accepted his condition. Paul not only accepted God's answer, but he understood the purpose for it remaining with him. He would not ask a fourth time.

We've now looked at two clearly defined stock market and biblical examples of the *Decision-Maker DNA* in action.

Could it be a coincidence?

It sure doesn't look like it.

Could there be more encounters in the Bible in which an event or answer is repeated three times and three times only?

Yes!

There are many more.

Let's look at a third example of the stock market and the Bible. After all, I couldn't really ask you to believe this after only seeing it two times.

Looking Back at the NASDAQ Composite in 1998: *The Triple Tank* — Part III

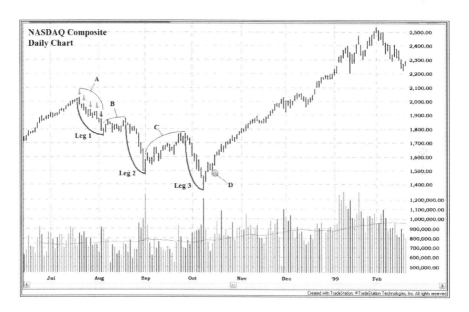

Here we go again!

- **POINT A**: Institutional selling stops the market in its tracks.

- **POINT B** is the short attempt to recover.

- It doesn't last long, and then you head down for **Leg 2**.

- **POINT C** makes you feel better but still doesn't pan out to be the end.

- **Leg 3** flushes the system as the *Decision-Maker DNA* comes to life, and out you go.

No way!

Not you!

Not now!

You're going to use this information to operate differently. No more stress. No more sitting with a loss because you bought at the wrong time. You'll be in at the right time, and you'll nail down a profit at the right time. No more guesswork!

MOSES AND THREE MIRACLES

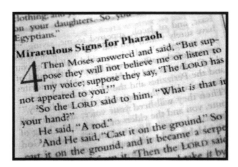

In Exodus, chapters 3 and 4, Moses encounters God and is appointed to deliver the people out of slavery. Moses feels inadequate and would appear to rather stay at home and let God find someone else.

God sees it differently and wants Moses to have confidence in Him, not in himself. God understands his concerns and provides him with a plan. The plan is to get the Pharaoh's attention using three different miracles.

This example is so powerful because it is God telling Moses how he can prove to others that God did, indeed, send him.

God knows our psychology. After all, He created us *and* the *Decision-Maker DNA*.

Instead of me paraphrasing, let's just read it straight from the Bible.

Exodus 4:1–12:

¹ *Moses answered, "What if they do not believe me or listen to me and say, 'The Lord did not appear to you'?"*

² *Then the Lord said to him, "What is that in your hand?"*

"A staff," he replied.

³ *The Lord said, "Throw it on the ground."*

Moses threw it on the ground, and it became a snake, and he ran from it.

⁴ *Then the Lord said to him, "Reach out your hand, and take it by the tail."*

So Moses reached out and took hold of the snake and it turned back into a staff in his hand.

⁵ *"This," said the Lord, "is so that they may believe that the Lord, the God of their fathers – the God of Abraham, the God of Isaac, and the God of Jacob – has appeared to you."* ⁶ *Then the Lord said, "Put your hand inside your cloak."*

So Moses put his hand into his cloak, and when he took it out, it was leprous, like snow.

⁷ *"Now put it back into your cloak," He said.*

So Moses put his hand back into his cloak, and when he took it out, it was restored, like the rest of his flesh.

⁸ **Then the Lord said, "If they do not believe you or pay attention to the first miraculous sign, they may believe the second.** ⁹ **But**

if they do not believe these two signs or listen to you, take some water from the Nile, and pour it on the dry ground. The water you take from the river will become blood on the ground."

[10] *Moses said to the Lord, "O Lord, I have never been eloquent, neither in the past, nor since you have spoken to your servant. I am slow of speech and tongue."*

[11] *The Lord said to him, "Who gave man his mouth? Who makes him deaf or mute? Who gives him sight or makes him blind? Is it not I, the Lord?* [12] *Now go; I will help you speak and will teach you what to say."*

It is amazing to see God, in verses 8 and 9, point out that even after two miracles, they still may not believe. He then gives Moses **a third miracle**.

If we are going to understand, accept, or believe, three times will do it. [1]

Of the many more examples of the *Decision-Maker DNA* at work in the Bible, a few others that you should study include: Jesus before Pilate (Luke 23), Jesus in Gethsemane (Matthew 26), and the temptation of Jesus (Matthew 4). I encourage you to read through all of these, and I'm certain you'll be amazed at the power of the *Decision-Maker DNA* and how frequently it occurs in the Bible. If you let the Bible come into your everyday life and you consider it diligently, it may let you see God in new ways and give you an even deeper admiration for who He is.

I hope you have gained an understanding of the *Decision-Maker DNA, The Triple Tank*, and how they affect you. As you can see, applying biblical principles to your everyday life can be a wonderful and valuable experience.

ONE STONE, ONE KILL

To a lot of people, the stock market has the stature of an undefeatable giant. The Bible has a great accounting of a young man, David, facing a rather intimidating giant, Goliath. David was not a well-trained soldier, armed with a semi-automatic rifle and hand grenades. He was simply a young man with a rather primitive tool, and he wasn't afraid to face off with a giant.

David defeated Goliath with a single stone.

Why is that relevant to you when you venture into the world of investing?

There are several key principles.

David didn't have a large stone and some fancy contraption that would catapult the stone. All he had was his own ability and a small stone, which was thrown using a sling—nothing fancy by any stretch of the imagination. What David did have was God on his side and the willingness to tackle a seemingly impossible task. He needed to defeat a giant. He had the skill, he believed that he could, and he was willing to try.

When it comes to investing, you also need to have great skills, believe in your abilities, and be willing to try.

How did David really defeat the giant?

He stood firm and used one stone, throwing with super accuracy.

He could have thought: *Well, let's see, I'll keep throwing stones as Goliath approaches me, and one will surely hit the mark.*

But he didn't.

He didn't count on using lots of stones and chancing the result. He threw one stone and put down a giant. He crushed the naysayers and skeptics in the crowd. Victory was his and God's.

The advantage of accuracy and well-timed effort is obvious in this story. When it comes to investing your money, you need to consider both of these.

One well-timed investment in the right place can make all the difference in the world.

To engage the stock market, you'll need courage and skills. You'll also need a stone. *The Triple Tank* will be that stone. It will provide the timing you need to eliminate risk and maximize gains.

Hitting the mark will be up to you.

While accuracy and great timing in the stock market may seem impossible, Matthew 19:26 tells us that "with God, all things are possible."

The Bible can change you, rebuild you, and make you better than you were before.

It reminds me of an old television program I loved as a kid: *The Six Million Dollar Man*.

Are you an investor, barely alive?

We can rebuild you. We have the technology. We have the capability to make the world's first bionic investor. We can make you better than you were before.

---

[1] Although three is the number needed to help us understand, accept, or believe, it isn't 100 percent foolproof. If you've studied your Bible, you know that while this was a good start for Moses, Pharaoh was tough, and it would take many, many more miracles before he would see the light of day. This is simply because God intended to do many more miracles to prove to the people who He was. Even *The Triple Tank* isn't 100 percent accurate, but it does prove to be beneficial for the vast majority of occasions on which it is encountered.

Want Proof?
The Triple Tank™

"The best way to show that a stick is crooked is not to argue about it or to spend time denouncing it, but to lay a straight stick alongside it."

~D.L. Moody

TRUTH OR THEORY?

In a courtroom, it doesn't matter what you think is true or even what you know is true. All that matters is what you can prove is true.

Why would you consider learning how to use the *Triple Tank System*?

Maybe it appears too good to be true or just a fancy theory.

The purpose of this chapter is to prove the realness and relevance of *The Triple Tank*, that it has been occurring since the beginning of the stock market and is the direct result of your *Decision-Maker DNA* and God's fingerprint on the financial markets. The following charts are the proof I discovered years ago, plus even more recent examples over the past several years, showing *The Triple Tank* in action.

Keep in mind that this is a small sample and is not an all-inclusive historical representation of *The Triple Tank*.

The purpose is to illustrate *The Triple Tank* occurring many times throughout history.

Please note that, due to the difficulty in charting stocks more than twenty-five years back, the individual stocks begin in 1991 and continue into 2014. The gains shown are not intended to mean that you could have made that gain. They are simply to show the result after *The Triple Tank* in the following six months. It is simply a six-month time frame for the stocks shown. Many of them gained more than what is shown within the six-month time period, and some went on to much bigger gains after the six months measured here. The shorter time frame for stocks in 2014 is due to the chart being current and including all available data as of this writing.

This information should *not* be viewed as a recommendation to buy *any investment*. It is for illustrative purposes to demonstrate *The Triple Tank* advantage.

You will see three variations of *The Triple Tank*:

1. *Powerhouse*

2. *Pause*

3. *Possum*

All have three declines and are very similar. The main differences involve the amount of time it takes for them to form and the percentage decline from the high. The *Possum* is almost exclusive to an index and can appear after any major market bottom.

The variations of the Triple Tank and the details of det
when to buy are fully explained in the *Triple Tank System*
Guide and Model Book available at:

www.RonTank.com

The important aspect of The Triple Tank is the reliability of
the gains that follow. Given their reliability, they present great
opportunities to leverage your money and create big gains in
a short period of time. Using The Triple Tank is like Warren
Buffett writing you a check.

As part of the FREE Book Bonus, you can download your 3
training videos by visiting: www.RonTank.com/BookBonus

These training videos were taken directly from my private
coaching program. They provide a detailed explanation of the
Triple Tank Powerhouse, Possum and Pause and will help you
more fully understand each one.

STOCK CHARTS

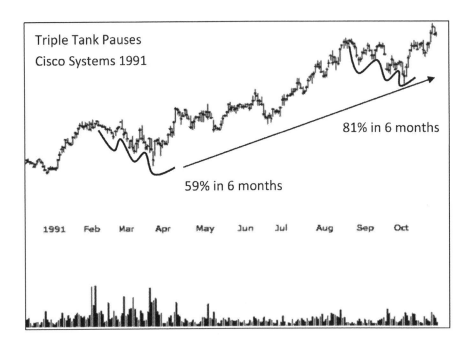

Triple Tank Pauses
Cisco Systems 1991

81% in 6 months

59% in 6 months

1991   Feb   Mar   Apr   May   Jun   Jul   Aug   Sep   Oct

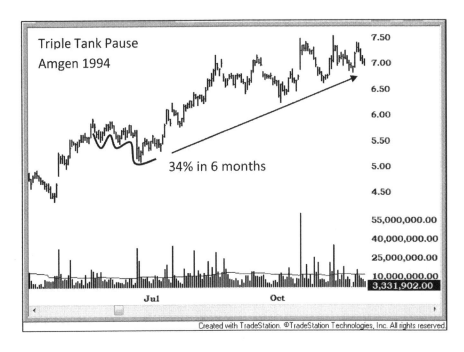

Triple Tank Pause
Amgen 1994

34% in 6 months

7.50
7.00
6.50
6.00
5.50
5.00
4.50

55,000,000.00
40,000,000.00
25,000,000.00
10,000,000.00
3,331,902.00

Jul   Oct

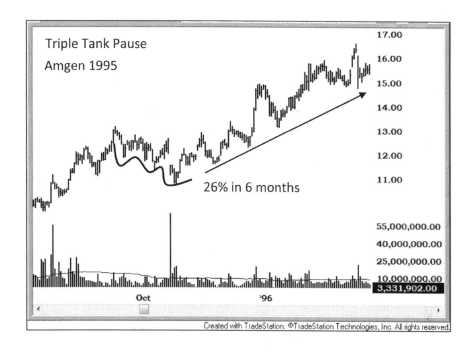

Triple Tank Pause
Amgen 1995

26% in 6 months

Oct   '96

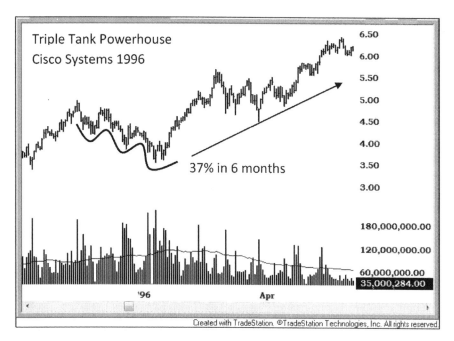

Triple Tank Powerhouse
Cisco Systems 1996

37% in 6 months

'96   Apr

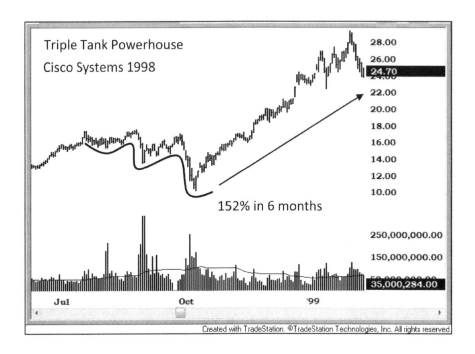

Triple Tank Powerhouse
Cisco Systems 1998

152% in 6 months

Created with TradeStation. ®TradeStation Technologies, Inc. All rights reserved.

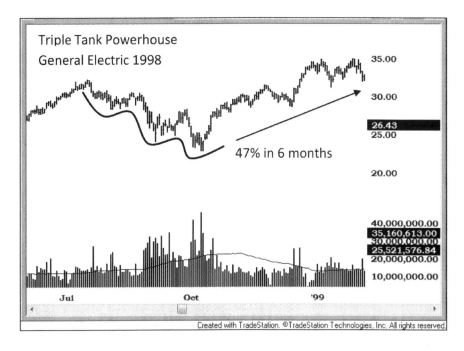

Triple Tank Powerhouse
General Electric 1998

47% in 6 months

Created with TradeStation. ®TradeStation Technologies, Inc. All rights reserved.

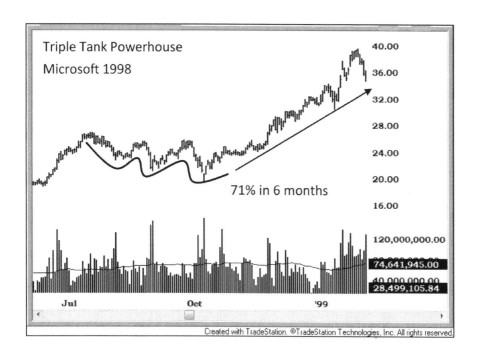

Triple Tank Powerhouse
Microsoft 1998

71% in 6 months

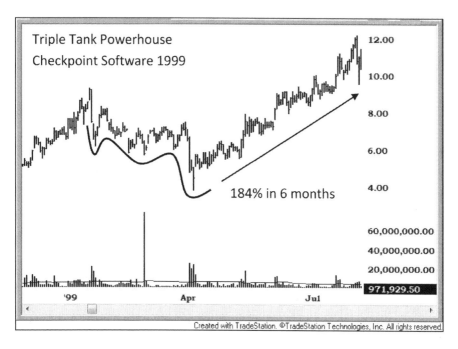

Triple Tank Powerhouse
Checkpoint Software 1999

184% in 6 months

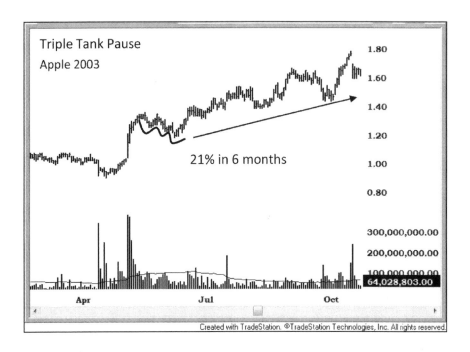

Triple Tank Pause
Apple 2003

21% in 6 months

Triple Tank Powerhouse
CME Group 2003

95% in 6 months

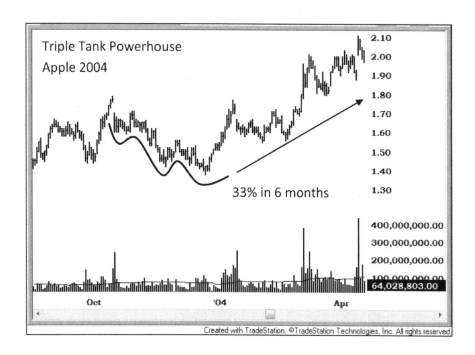

Triple Tank Powerhouse
Apple 2004

33% in 6 months

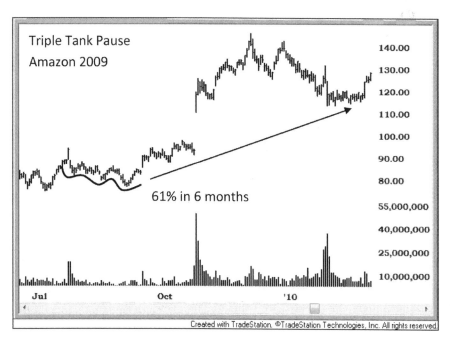

Triple Tank Pause
Amazon 2009

61% in 6 months

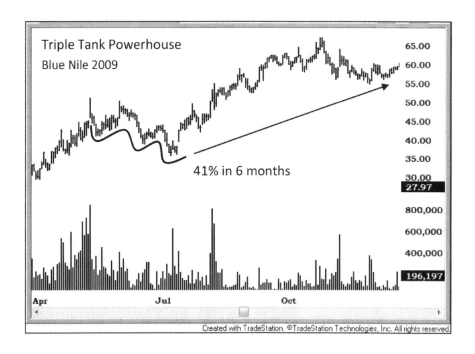

Triple Tank Powerhouse
Blue Nile 2009

41% in 6 months

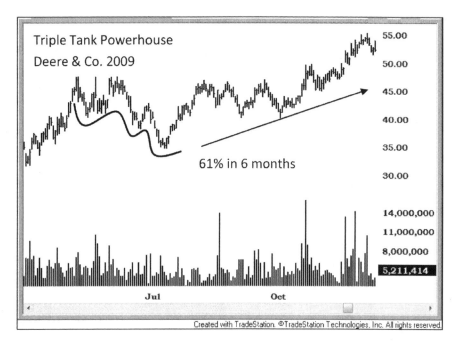

Triple Tank Powerhouse
Deere & Co. 2009

61% in 6 months

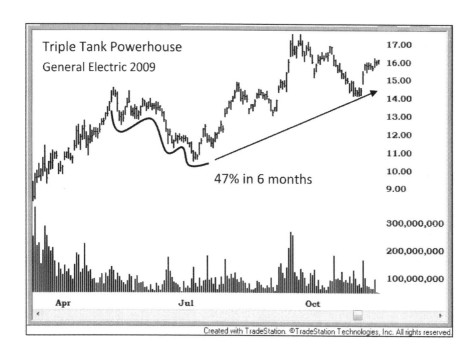

Triple Tank Powerhouse
General Electric 2009

47% in 6 months

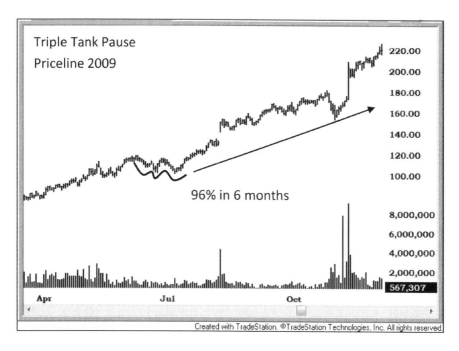

Triple Tank Pause
Priceline 2009

96% in 6 months

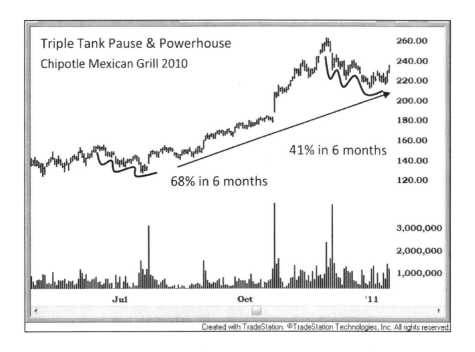

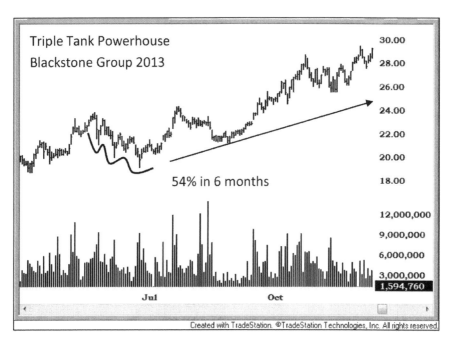

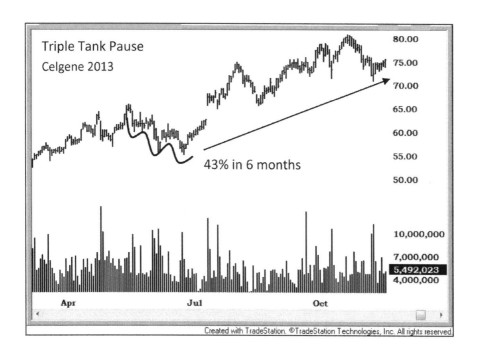

Triple Tank Pause
Celgene 2013

43% in 6 months

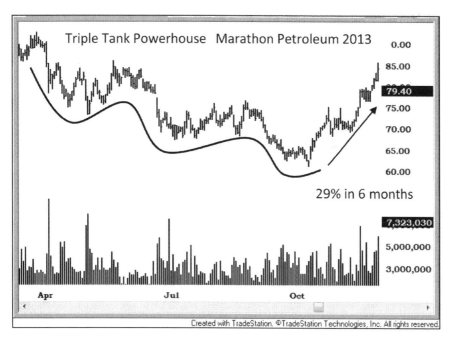

Triple Tank Powerhouse   Marathon Petroleum 2013

79.40

29% in 6 months

7,323,030

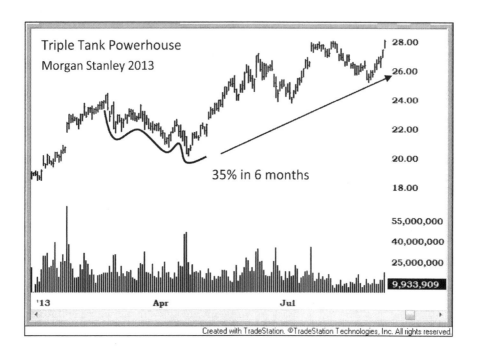

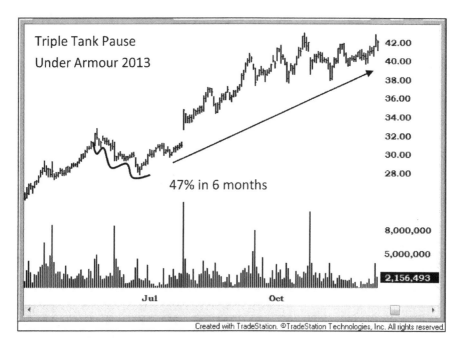

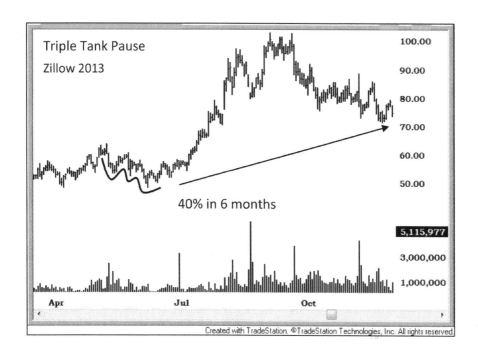

Triple Tank Pause
Zillow 2013

40% in 6 months

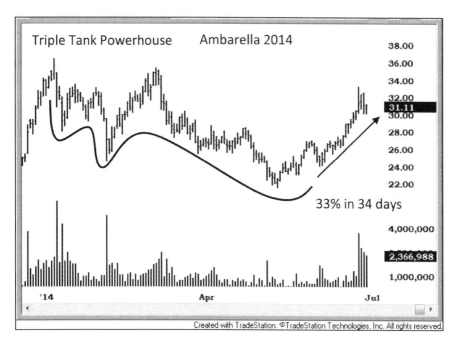

Triple Tank Powerhouse   Ambarella 2014

33% in 34 days

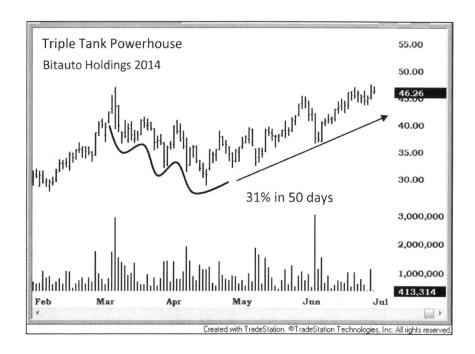

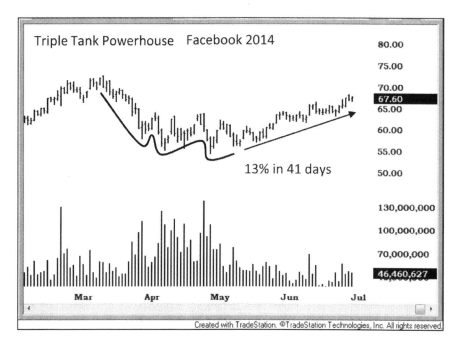

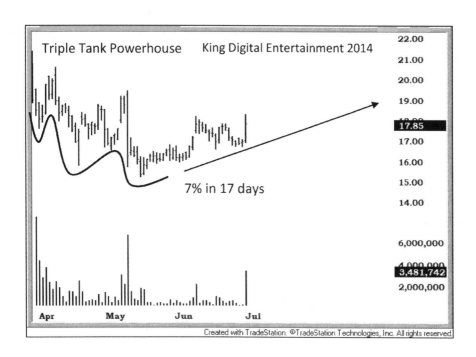

Triple Tank Powerhouse   King Digital Entertainment 2014

7% in 17 days

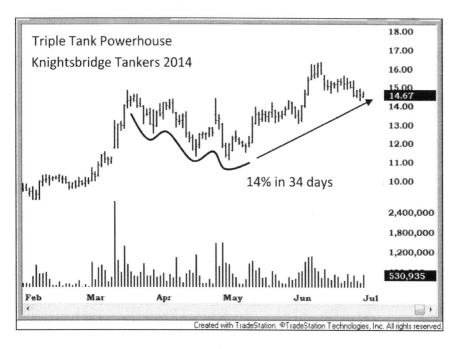

Triple Tank Powerhouse
Knightsbridge Tankers 2014

14% in 34 days

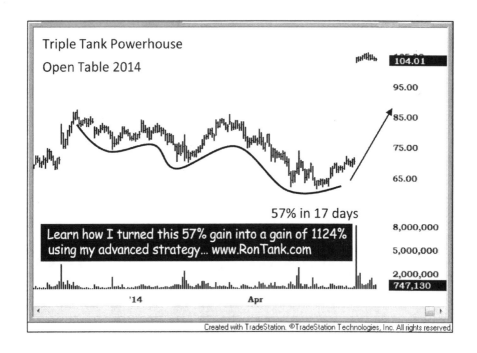

Triple Tank Powerhouse
Open Table 2014

57% in 17 days

Learn how I turned this 57% gain into a gain of 1124% using my advanced strategy... www.RonTank.com

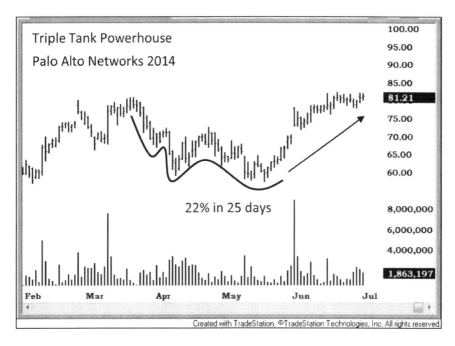

Triple Tank Powerhouse
Palo Alto Networks 2014

22% in 25 days

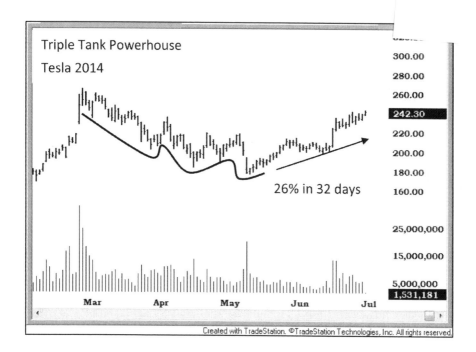

As part of the FREE Book Bonus, you can download your Special Report, The Triple Tank Stocks Update, by visiting: www.RonTank.com/BookBonus

This report contains Triple Tanks occurring after the book was published and are great models to study and learn from.

INDEX CHARTS

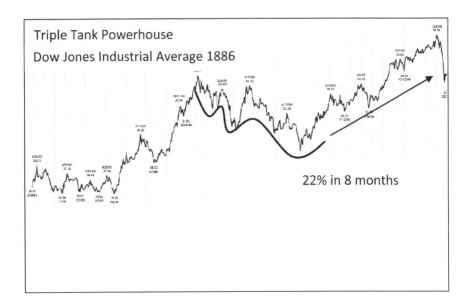

Triple Tank Powerhouse
Dow Jones Industrial Average 1886

22% in 8 months

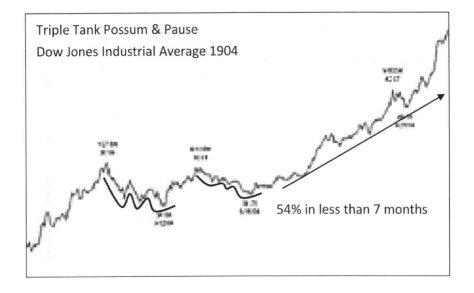

Triple Tank Possum & Pause
Dow Jones Industrial Average 1904

54% in less than 7 months

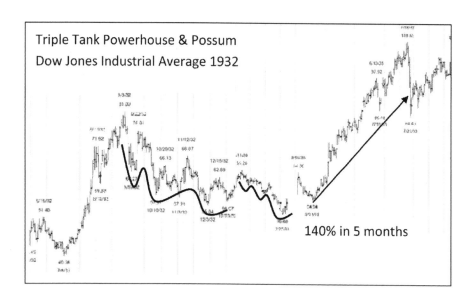

Triple Tank Powerhouse & Possum
Dow Jones Industrial Average 1932

140% in 5 months

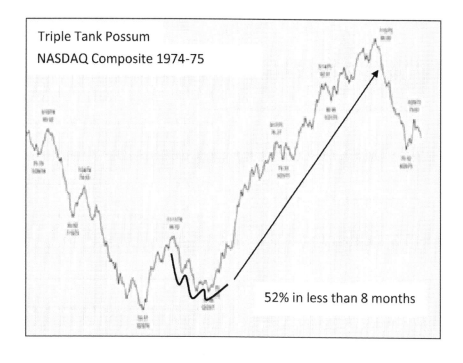

Triple Tank Possum
NASDAQ Composite 1974-75

52% in less than 8 months

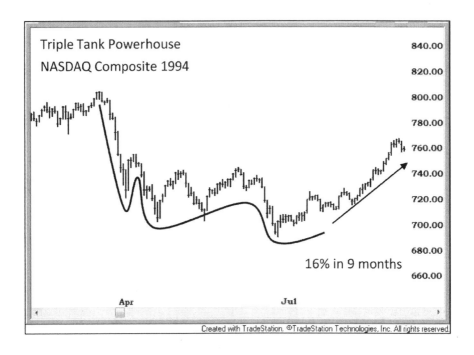

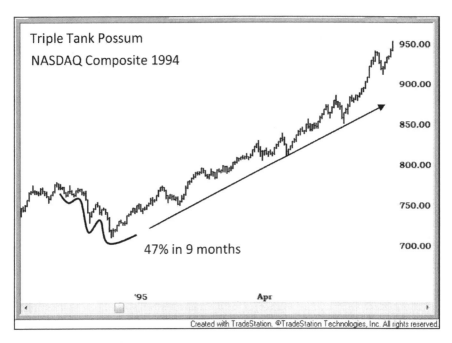

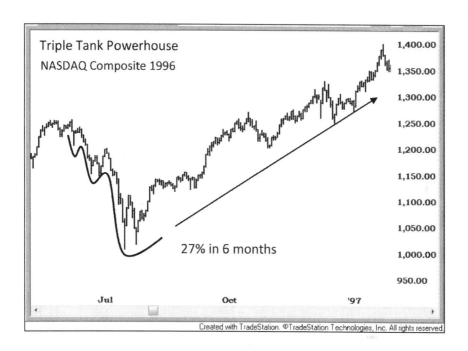

Triple Tank Powerhouse
NASDAQ Composite 1996

27% in 6 months

Triple Tank Powerhouse
NASDAQ Composite 1998

228% in 1 year 5 months

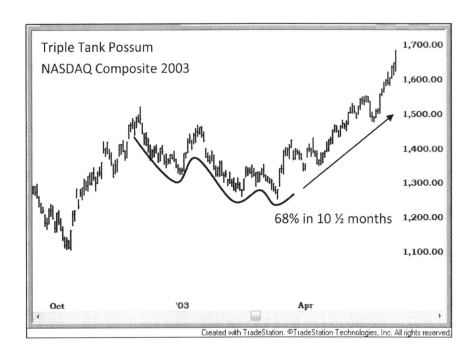

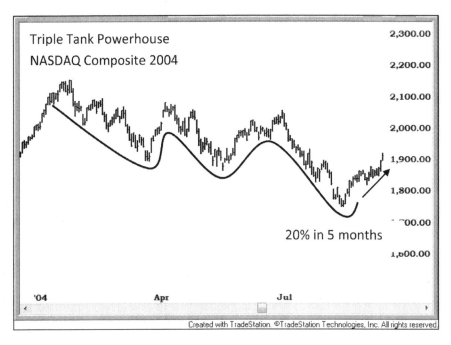

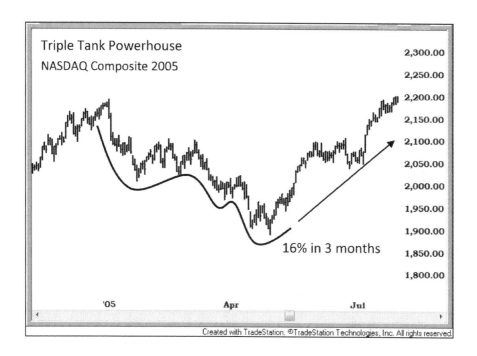

Triple Tank Powerhouse
NASDAQ Composite 2005

16% in 3 months

Triple Tank Powerhouse
NASDAQ Composite 2005 Fall

14% in 6 months

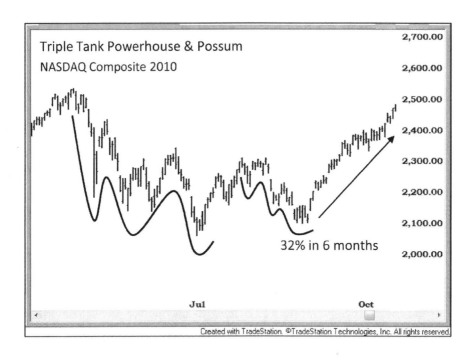

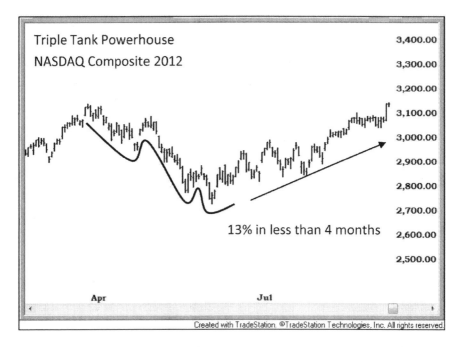

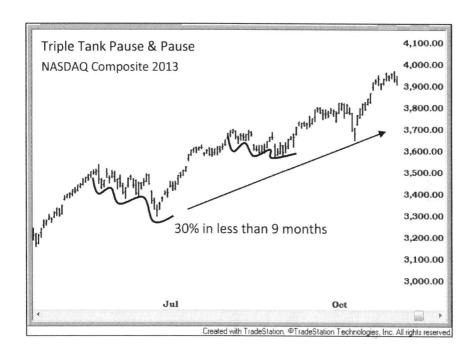

Triple Tank Pause & Pause
NASDAQ Composite 2013

30% in less than 9 months

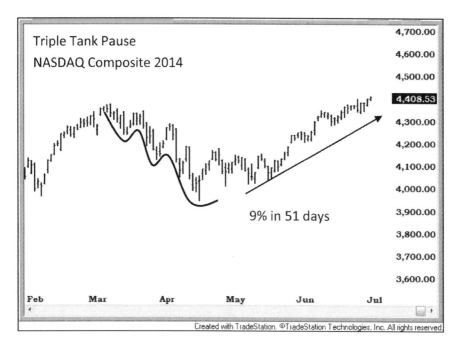

Triple Tank Pause
NASDAQ Composite 2014

9% in 51 days

As part of the FREE Book Bonus, you can download your
Special Report, The Triple Tank Stocks Update, by visiting:
www.RonTank.com/BookBonus

***This report contains Triple Tanks occurring after the book was
published and are great models to study and learn from.***

One Deadly Sin You Must Avoid: News, You Lose!

"If you don't read the newspaper, you're uninformed. If you read the newspaper, you're misinformed."

~*(attributed to) Mark Twain*

The news will never guide you to a good investment decision.

To the individual, the news can be helpful at times. News of an impending hurricane or a tornado sweeping across the country can be crucial information. Our world is very dynamic, and events being reported to us accurately, in real time, can be valuable to us.

At the same time, it's essential that you understand the role played by the news media and how it appears to affect the markets. Generally, the news is about bad things happening and will serve to scare you to death. I have never heard of a successful stock market strategy based on the reporting of news. Most often, the news media fail to recognize what the financial markets consistently foretell: that a change for the better is just ahead.

In order to see the change for the better happening, you'll need to learn how to interpret a chart of the indexes, which is what real people are doing with real money on any given day. The news is based on what *has* happened. Financial markets move on what *will* happen. The advance in the financial markets has a peculiar way of stopping right about the time when everyone is really beginning to have confidence and the news is sounding promising.

All good things must come to an end, right?

The ascent of the major stock market indexes stops, turns south, and commences to decline. It never feels real at first. The news media begin to talk about all the reasons why it should be going down. After many weeks or months, the news continues to tell you exactly why you should be concerned. The market continues down, and the popular news of the day just keeps getting uglier and uglier. Somehow, every pundit on television has the answer for why the market is up or down on any given day.

You can just imagine what will happen next. The longer the market has been going down, the more likely it is that the news is getting worse and worse, seemingly justifying the market's downward spiral. The news will constantly remind you about one cold, hard fact: *You are getting killed in the stock market!* Everything appears to be crumbling. Eventually, the news on television will tell you that the world is about to end: *Armageddon has arrived!*

Several years back, Art Cashin — a very smart and colorful man on the floor of the New York Stock Exchange — had a great response to the carnage in the stock market. He said something to this effect: It won't pay you to short the markets based on the end of the world coming because it will only happen once.

I agree.

Even if you're right, who's going to care?

While the media are pounding you with all the reasons why the world is coming to an end, your *Decision-Maker DNA* is working to confirm what you are hearing and seeing. After taking a severe beating for many months, you are wearing thin. You may have sold out of the stock market altogether—right smack-dab at the bottom of *The Triple Tank.*

I hope not.

If you have, it shouldn't happen to you anymore.

The worst of the news will not stop the stock market from finding bottom and beginning a whole new advance.

You must exit the market when the warning signs are there and come back after the bottom is reached in *The Triple Tank. The Triple Tank* is rock bottom.

Some may claim this sounds like bottom fishing. I strongly disagree. It is bottom *catching.* There is a big difference. If you're like me, when you go fishing, you like catching fish.

The markets will get better, but the news often continues to remain desperate for many weeks, or even months, after the bottom has come. The news will promote doom and gloom, but the market will not wait for the news to get better and will leave you behind if you are waiting for the news to sound promising.

News, you lose.

A PROVEN METHOD

Now, we're going to look at some charts of market troubles from years gone by. We'll observe the news and discover why it will only serve to derail you in the stock market. The value of a proven method will become obvious.

I'll follow Churchill's advice once again as we look at three examples. (I'm really using your *Decision-Maker DNA* to help you understand and believe.)

In the first example, the NASDAQ had declined over 36 percent in seventeen days during the crash of 1987, found bottom, n advanced rather normally until the hard break that occurred in October of 1989. By the end of October, 1989, the NASDAQ was signaling that another top was at hand.

I strongly suggest that you review the events in more detail for the years of 1988 through 1991. If you already have the *Triple Tank System* Strategy Guide and Model Book, you can open up the model book and review it while viewing all of the examples in this chapter.

Get the *Triple Tank System* Strategy Guide and Model Book at:

www.RonTank.com

Here, we'll focus more on the news at critical times and on what the market was doing around those major news events.

The NASDAQ Composite in 1990–91

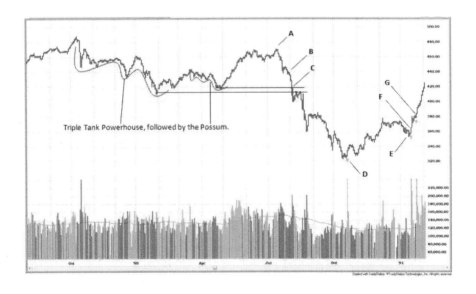

POINT A: The market is acting very normally until this point in mid-July.

POINT B: On August 2, Iraq invades Kuwait. There are concerns over the US oil supply.

POINT C: Institutional selling in the NASDAQ confirms a market top. *Leave now.*

POINT D: On October 18, the market confirms its bottom with a classic O'Neil Follow-Through Rally.[1] The market has declined by 31 percent from **POINT A** in July.

POINT E: On Saturday, January 12, the US Congress votes for war against Iraq.

POINT F: On Wednesday, January 16, Operation Desert Storm begins. The market has a *Big Day*[2] up, confirming that the *Possum*,[2] having lasted several weeks, has ended.

POINT G: On Wednesday, January 23, a second Follow-Through Rally confirms that the *Possum* is really dead. *Go! Go! Go!*

Notice how the NASDAQ responded to the news of the Iraqi invasion at point B. A big, ugly, nasty war was about to threaten the US. We would encounter huge losses, sky-high oil prices, and as a result, our economy would take a huge hit, according to the news.

Or maybe not.

In less than three months, the market assessed the situation and decided that the opportunities here at home were very real. The doom and gloom was nothing but smoke.

Selling out is always good if the *market* tells you to. But listening to the *news*, expecting Armageddon, and staying out is just bad thinking.

Following a proven method to find a market bottom is much wiser thinking.

Sir John Templeton once said, "Bull markets are born on pessimism, grow on skepticism, mature on optimism, and die on euphoria."

Microsoft, Cisco Systems, and many others were coming alive in the market and moving up strong after this point in time. They would go on to massive gains during the technology and internet revolution over the next ten years.

If you let the news dictate your investment decisions, you'll likely be doing the wrong thing at the wrong time—and likely for the wrong reasons.

News, you lose.

The NASDAQ Composite in 1998

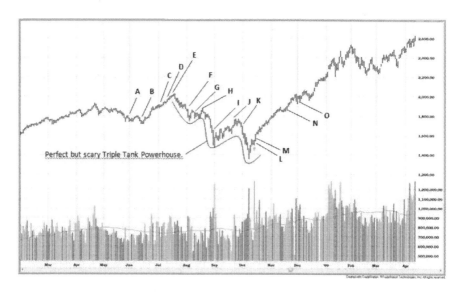

POINT A: On June 1, 1998, Russia's stock market crashes, and Moscow's cash reserves dwindle to $14 billion amid unsuccessful attempts to prop up the ruble and pay off burgeoning debts. President Clinton pledges support for Yeltsin. [3]

POINT B: On June 12, 1998, Japan announces that its economy is in a recession for the first time in twenty-three years.[3]

POINT C: On July 6, 1998, Moscow's markets get pummeled as the government fails to raise cash by selling government shares of a state-owned oil company. Moscow hints that an IMF loan agreement is near. [3]

POINT D: On July 13, 1998, the IMF announces $23 billion of emergency loans for Russia. The international lender dips into an emergency line of credit to provide its share of financing. Russian stocks and bonds soar. [3]

POINT E: On July 20, 1998, the IMF gives final approval to a $22.6 billion loan package to Russia.[3]

POINT F: Institutional selling confirms that the NASDAQ market is topped and in trouble.

POINT G: On August 11, 1998, the Russian market collapses. Trading on the stock market is temporarily suspended. World markets are rocked by fears of a financial meltdown in Asia and Russia. [3]

POINT H: On August 19, 1998, Russia fails to pay its debt on GKO treasury bills, thereby officially falling into default. The IMF and G7 say they won't provide additional loans to Russia until it meets existing promises.[3]

POINT I: On August 31, 1998, after weeks of decline, Wall Street is overwhelmed by the turmoil in Russia and world markets. The Dow Jones Industrial Average plunges 512 points—the second-worst point loss in the Dow's history.[3]

POINT J: On Sept. 23, 1998, pushed by the Federal Reserve Bank of New York, a consortium of leading US financial institutions provides a $3.6 billion bailout to Long-Term Capital Management, one of the largest US hedge funds, amidst fears that a collapse could worsen the panic in the financial markets. [3]

POINT K: On Sept. 30, 1998, worries that the Fed isn't doing enough to rescue the US and global economies cause a 238-point drop in the Dow, for a loss of more than 500 points in a week. Investors around the world flock to US Treasury bonds for safety, causing the yield on thirty-year bonds to drop below 5 percent for the first time in three decades. [3]

POINT L: On Oct. 14, 1998, an O'Neil Follow-Through Rally confirms that the market is now up.

POINT M: On Oct. 15, 1998, to prevent weak financial markets from tripping the US into a recession, the Fed cuts interest rates for a second time. The Dow shoots up 331 points, and world markets rally. [3]

POINT N: On Nov. 17, 1998, citing "unusual strains" in the credit markets, the Fed cuts interest rates for the third time in seven weeks. [3]

POINT O: On Dec. 2, 1998, the World Bank projects that the crisis has cut world growth in half, to around 2 percent, and that unless Japan reverses the decline of its economy, the world could fall into recession in 1999. [3]

I remember this time period very well. There were many stocks that were in base patterns and acting very well — almost as if, somehow, the shareholders knew that the bell was going to ring and the horse race would commence.

That is exactly what happened, and I made the biggest gain of my career — *more than 5,000 percent in just under one-and-a-half years, turning $40,000 into $2.2 million. I started at the very bottom of The Triple Tank in October, 1998.*

Beginning in mid-October, after the Follow-Through Rally, many stocks left the starting gates and never looked back. Six weeks after the bottom, the World Bank still didn't have a clue.

Sometimes, conventional thinking can be wrong — and costly.

It reminds me of what Mark Twain said a long time ago, "It ain't what you don't know that gets you into trouble. It's what you know for sure that just ain't so."

I suspect that a lot of people bailed out based on all the Armageddon news. By the first few days of August, the NASDAQ and other indexes were broadcasting trouble by their behavior, regardless of the news. By mid-October, the NASDAQ flashed the signal that all was well.

If you learn to listen to the market, all the bad news the media can and will throw at you won't matter one bit. If you let the news make you believe that this time is different and you must sell and stay out to avoid the coming calamity, just remember:

News, you lose.

After the previous two examples, you might be asking again, "Why not just stay in there and never sell out?"

The answer is that, one day, you'll run into a big bear like the one lasting from 2000 to 2003. We'll look at the bottom of that monster bear market next.

Talking about bears reminds me of the two guys who were packing to go moose hunting in Alaska when one noticed the other packing a pair of running shoes along with his hunting gear.

Curious, he asked, "What are the running shoes for?"

"In case I run into a bear."

Puzzled, he then asked, "How are the shoes going to help you outrun the bear?"

"I don't have to outrun the bear. I only have to outrun you!"

Wouldn't you rather run than face off with a bear?

In the markets, you'll never know it's a bear until long after you should have run.

The NASDAQ Composite in 2003

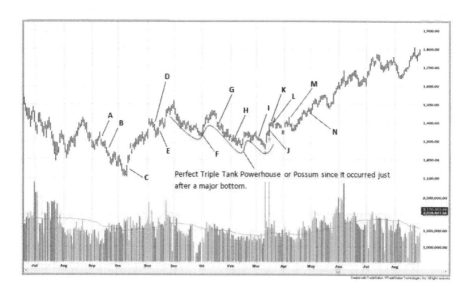

POINT A: On September 12, 2002, President Bush remarks to the UN General Assembly concerning Iraq.

POINT B: On September 19, 2002, President Bush to send Iraq Resolution to Congress.

POINT C: On October 10, 2002, Congress authorizes Bush to use force against Iraq. *At the low of this day, the NASDAQ had declined by 78 percent from March of 2000.*

POINT D: On November 8, 2002, The United Nations Security Council unanimously approves a resolution on Iraq, forcing Saddam Hussein to disarm or face "serious consequences."

POINT E: On November 13, 2002, Iraq agrees to the terms of UN Security Council Resolution 1441.

POINT F: On January 1, 2003, the first twenty-five thousand US troops start deploying to the Persian Gulf region.

POINT G: On January 20, 2003, one week before Hans Blix's first major report to the council, French Foreign Minister Dominique de Villepin blindsides the United States at a UN press conference, saying that France will oppose any move toward war.

POINT H: On February 5, 2003, Colin Powell addresses the Security Council and presents the case for force against Saddam Hussein's regime.

POINT I: On March 5, 2003, more than two hundred thousand US troops, five carrier groups and one thousand aircraft are in place or en route to the Middle East. France and Russia pledge to veto any resolution authorizing force. Two days later, the British begin a final effort at diplomacy.

POINT J: On March 17, 2003, a NASDAQ Follow-Through Rally confirms that a new bull market has begun. President Bush issues an ultimatum to Saddam, giving him forty-eight hours to leave the country or face war.

POINT K: On March 19, 2003, cruise-missile and bomb salvos hit Baghdad an hour after the deadline passes. Operation Iraqi Freedom begins without United Nations support and in defiance of world opinion.

POINT L: On March 23, 2003, in Nasiriyah, Iraq, eleven soldiers of the 507th Maintenance Company as well as eighteen US Marines are killed during the first major conflict of Operation Iraqi Freedom.

POINT M: On April 7, 2003, US troops capture Baghdad. Saddam Hussein's regime falls two days later.

POINT N: On May 1, 2003, President George W. Bush declares that "major combat operations in Iraq have ended" on board the USS Abraham Lincoln off the coast of California in what becomes known as the "Mission Accomplished" speech.

If you got caught up in the news of despair due to the events surrounding the Iraq war in 1990–91, the foreign markets and Long-Term Capital Management in 1998, and the Iraq war once again in 2003, then you might have missed some great opportunities in the markets.

These are just a few of the many times news has caused enough fear to seriously impact the financial lives of many, many people. The news is often packed with disheartening events. Tragedy and despair can keep us in fear and influence us in making bad decisions. Experts continually appear to have all the answers as to why the stock market goes up and down when times are scary. Everyone wants an answer to explain the terrible times.

Rest assured, an O'Neil Follow-Through Rally occurring after a *Triple Tank Powerhouse, Possum or Pause*[4] is as good as money in the bank, regardless of the news at the time.

The teachings of history have incredible value — more than you might ever imagine — in helping you identify *The Triple Tank*. The NASDAQ Composite *Triple Tank* in 1974–75 is a twin of the 2003 *Triple Tank* bottom. (You'll find a chart of the 1974–75 *Triple Tank* in the *Triple Tank* System Model Book.) Another bottom in the future will look very similar. The *Triple Tank System* Model Book has tremendous value in training your eye to spot a diamond that most other investors will never see.

What could it be worth to you?

Are you ready for the *Triple Tank System*?

It will show you what to do and how to do it, and it will let you sleep at night.

Go to:

www.RonTank.com

If you've been beaten up and knocked down in the past, it's important to remember that it happens to everyone at times in life. The getting up part, though, is up to you.

Allowing the news to influence your decision to put money in or take money out of the stock market is the one deadly sin you must avoid.

News, you lose!

Follow a system and win.

---

[1] O'Neil Follow-Through Rally is a term coined by William J. O'Neil in his book, *How to Make Money in Stocks*, and also used in the *Triple Tank System* Strategy Guide and Model Book.

[2] Big Day, Triple Tank Powerhouse, Possum, and Pause are terms coined by Ron Tank and used in the *Triple Tank System* Strategy Guide and Model Book.

[3] This passage was excerpted from WGBH Educational Foundation's *Frontline®* episode, "The Crash: Unraveling the 1998 Global Financial Crisis...Is the Worst Over?" at www.pbs.org/wgbh/pages/frontline/shows/crash/etc/cron.html.

[4] See note 2 above.

Three Keys to Becoming a Good and Faithful Servant (and Four Deadly Traps to Avoid)

"But be sure to fear the Lord and serve him faithfully with all your heart; consider what great things he has done for you."

~*1 Samuel 12:24*

In order to gain more and become a good and faithful servant, there are three keys you must possess and four deadly traps that must be avoided. How you answer several questions will determine where you are on the path.

Can you learn to put aside fear, have faith, and master the task of gaining more?

Can you avoid the trap of having "too much money"?

Can you have a generous heart and avoid greed and falling in love with money?

Do you desire to be rich in God, loving Him with all your heart, soul, and mind?

Will you be a slave to money or a servant of God?

DEADLY TRAP NUMBER ONE: Remaining in Fear

The fear of losing can be, and most often is, greater than the hope of gain. Most people would rather not gain than be exposed to risk and lose.

This is a healthy fear. It can lead to wisdom.

Warren Buffett says, "Risk comes from not knowing what you're doing."

To eliminate the risk, you need to gain knowledge and wisdom. The two will aid in your understanding and ability to take action.

Another fear you may have is one of being wrong.

The mere thought of being wrong and losing money can cause everything short of pure panic. That is what you may perceive to be the problem.

The real problem is not losing your money, which you can prevent if you choose to. You are really afraid of yourself. It is the fear of your *inability to act* and prevent a big loss that scares you.

Most people who are wrong in the market become long-term investors.

By admitting that a problem exists (you're losing money) and taking action quickly, you can prevent losses from becoming devastating. Fearing yourself and the lack of a disciplined plan to handle your losses — that is where risk is born.

✳ **The stock market will only do to you that which you allow.**

KNOWLEDGE, WISDOM, AND BELIEF

Faith and fear cannot coexist. One or the other is in control. One wins at any given moment, while the other must remain silent.

The Bible tells us in Psalm 111:10, "The fear of the Lor beginning of wisdom."

Does that mean we should be afraid of God and avoid Him?

Absolutely not.

Actually, quite the opposite.

To fear Him means that we have a healthy respect for Him. The respect originates in our hearts, and the result is that we should have a desire to gain more wisdom about Him.

Fear should lead to wisdom.

Knowledge is often defined as knowing what to do. Often, we find ourselves knowing we should do something, but we don't do it.

Sometimes, we discover something through other people's advice. Maybe a book gives us some knowledge as to what we should do.

We can, and often do, commit to an idea of what to do.

The problem that follows is: *Now that I know what I should do, how do I do it?*

Wisdom provides the "how" that is a necessary ingredient to accomplishing anything important to us. It is the key that unlocks knowledge, making it useful. It helps define the steps, so we can implement the knowledge we have.

The bad news is that we can have knowledge and wisdom and still do nothing.

This equation contains what is required:

$$(knowledge + wisdom^{believed} \times action = desired\ result)$$

The key to the equation is the word, "believed."

✳ Knowledge and wisdom produce nothing in idle hands.

Without belief, even the most powerful knowledge and wisdom can be absolutely worthless. We may go through the motions, but at times, our hearts are just not in it. We aren't sold on it.

We may not believe that part of the knowledge or wisdom is true. Or maybe we believe that the result will not occur. We must believe in the knowledge and wisdom, and we must also believe that the desired result is forthcoming.

Belief is the bridge that lets us cross over every excuse stopping us from moving forward. It leads us into the best possible mindset—one in which action leads to results. There are two doors at the entrance to the bridge of belief.

Door number one is fear. Fear can lead into the darkroom where negatives are developed. Fear can derail our best intentions. Fear can also be useful. It is signaling that we lack wisdom. We need to more fully understand what it is we are afraid of. Once we have a better understanding, the fear will dissipate. We may fear snakes. Some snakes are deadly while others won't hurt a flea.

But which are the deadly ones?

By gaining more knowledge and wisdom of how to identify and handle certain snakes, we can reduce the perceived harm and reduce our fear. Then the darkroom will go away.

Door number two is faith. We have passed through the door of fear, and we have chosen to let it guide us to wisdom, not to the darkroom. Armed with knowledge and wisdom, we must now pass through the door of faith. Faith has the power to deliver us into an eternal heavenly home. It also has the power to lead us into endeavors we would never undertake here on Earth.

Faith is defined by Hebrews 11:1, "Now faith is confidence in what we hope for and assurance of what we do not see."

Faith allows us to take one step without knowing all the steps. Faith gives us confidence — enough so that we will take action.

How do we have confidence in what we hope for and assurance of what we do not see?

Faith requires us to believe something as true. We must believe.

But isn't the secret to believing knowing whether something is true or just an opinion?

An opinion is a belief that is not substantiated by proof or evidence. A belief substantiated by proof or evidence becomes truth, not opinion.

Wouldn't faith lead us into a place where we have confidence, allowing us to take action, and the action would lead to a desired result?

KEY NUMBER ONE: Faith

When Christ sent out His disciples, He gave them lots of power.

He told them in Matthew 10:7-8, "As you go, proclaim this message: 'The kingdom of heaven has come near.' Heal the sick, raise the dead, cleanse those who have leprosy, drive out demons. Freely you have received; freely give."

Later (in chapter 17, verses 14-20), when the disciples could not free a boy of demons, Jesus ended up doing it himself.

When the disciples asked Him why they could not do it, Jesus replied, "Because you have so little faith. Truly I tell you, if you have faith as small as a mustard seed, you can say to this mountain, 'Move from here to there,' and it will move. Nothing will be impossible for you."

The disciples' one big problem was that they had been obedient, not faithful. The disciples were missing the "believed" part of the equation mentioned earlier. They really did not believe they could do what Jesus had given them the power to do, and therefore, they could not. They were simply going through the motions without believing in the result.

Obedience without faith is like the cross without Christ.

In Matthew 13:58, we are told that Jesus did not do many miracles in his home town.

Why didn't He do many miracles?

We know it wasn't because of his inability to do them. It doesn't say it was because He didn't want to do them. We are told it was because of *their* lack of faith.

If we want big things to happen, we must believe.

Henry Ford once said, "Whether you think you can or think you can't, you're right."

Belief is a powerful thing.

Noah built an ark. He was given, by God, the knowledge and wisdom needed to build it. He believed—or he had faith—in what God had told him, which was the truth.

What was the proof that rain would come?

He sure didn't have Doppler radar on his iPad.

His belief was rooted in his understanding of God. He had the wisdom and knowledge, and he believed God. Noah had assurance of that which couldn't be seen. He had faith, which resulted in action. His actions led to the survival of his family, the animals, and mankind.

I'll bet that Noah was a little scared of the coming rain. It's likely that he was even more scared of his responsibility to build a gigantic ark. But his faith in God and the wisdom he received annihilated any fear.

We will encounter fear, and it can be healthy if we acknowledge its presence, discover the knowledge and wisdom we need, and believe.

Ultimately, we'll have faith. Faith causes us to see that which can't be seen, propelling us into action.

Fear remains in the darkroom, all by itself.

We have faith and do something, or we remain in fear and do nothing.

DEADLY TRAP NUMBER TWO: Too Much Money

I remember growing up thinking that money was the grandest of them all. If you had lots of money, you were a king.

You could have a big house with lots of nice things inside, a nice car to drive to work, and the best food (or at least, the food you wanted to eat instead of what you could afford).

We lived in an average house for the rural area at the time. Although some neighbors thought we had it made in the shade.

The strange thing I remember is that, on more than one occasion, through casual conversations with other people, I would hear my dad comment about money not growing on trees and about how hard he worked in order for us to have the things we did.

I thought we were pretty well off, but at the same time, if a neighbor commented on how nice it must be to have money, my dad would act as if he was barely getting by. I never really understood whether or not he was living on the edge of not being able to pay for what we had.

Was it that we did have a lot, and my dad just felt guilty for having it—almost denying we had nice things because money was not a good thing to have?

Could it be possible to have too much money?

I always thought the obvious answer was, "No way!"

As a young boy, I may have been right, but if I was, it was for all the wrong reasons.

You may have a tendency to feel guilty, believing you have too much money.

But what is too much money?

And why would you feel guilty for having money?

Are you afraid of falling in love with it?

To defeat this fear, you may think: *Well, I'm going to be satisfied with what I have. I don't need more.*

You must be careful that "satisfied" isn't just an excuse to be lazy and give in to the fear you experience when attempting to gain more.

God gives us a responsibility to do well with all that He gives us. If you think you have too much money, then your focus is likely on yourself or on the money instead of on God.

After all, why couldn't you use some of the money for good causes to which God directs you?

This would demonstrate generosity and help keep you in balance. You can avoid a heart that falls in love with money by constantly giving to God's church and other causes He brings to your attention.

KEY NUMBER TWO: A Generous Heart

Try this exercise:

- Imagine yourself standing upright with each arm extended straight out.

- God puts money in your right hand.

- Your hand clenches up into a fist and comes into your chest, as if to protect it.

- The money is now close to your heart.

Or is it?

If your heart loves the money, it will stay there. None of it will leave your hand.

If you are right in your relationship with God and view money as His, some of it will be allowed to leave.

In this case:

- Your left hand comes into your chest to meet the right hand over your heart.

- Your right hand gladly releases a portion of the money it is holding to your left hand.

- Once the money is transferred to your left hand, your left arm is extended straight out once again.

- Then your left hand opens and allows the money to depart, demonstrating that you'll allow money to pass through you to causes that God will show you.

God expects us to use our abilities for Him without ceasing.

While the world likes retirement, God expects lifetime stewardship.

God never intended for money and things to become our ultimate goal for achieving satisfaction in life.

Howard Hughes may have disagreed. He was once asked how much money it would take for someone to be happy.

He replied, "Just a little bit more."

Money is important.

Russell H. Conwell, author of the famous essay, *Acres of Diamonds*, said, "Money printed your Bible, money builds your churches, money sends your missionaries, and money pays your preachers, and you would not have many of them, either, if you did not pay them."

Once again, if you believe that you have too much money, it more than likely indicates that you are focused too much on the "I" part of "I don't need more."

Maybe you're not being generous, or you're getting greedy.

Could your focus be completely wrong?

Your focus needs to shift from you back to God and what He wants for you. You must truly believe that everything belongs to God. It is all His, and you have the responsibility of being a good steward, or manager.

The second half of Luke 12:48 says, "From everyone who has been given much, much will be demanded; and from the one who has been entrusted with much, much more will be asked."

Much can definitely come from God. And when it does, much will be asked.

So why ask whether you or others have too much?

How much is too much?

I don't believe we should concern ourselves with these questions. I do believe that if you tie your happiness to how much or how little money you have, you'll never be happy. And that is a big problem.

The real questions are:

How much of a good steward are you with what He has given you?

Will you focus on yourself and say that you have enough, or will you focus on Him and gain more?

Will He say, "Well done, good and faithful servant"?

DEADLY TRAP NUMBER THREE: Greed and Falling in Love with Money

Greed loves money.

I believe that greed and the love of money are relatives. Neither can get very far from the other. Somehow, our world has married high levels of income or big bank accounts to success. We want to be successful, so we chase after money and bigger and better things.

Having money and nice things isn't a sin.

Albert Einstein once said, *"Try not to become a man of success, but rather try to become a man of value."*

But what about the pursuit of money and other things at the expense of our relationship with God...wouldn't that separate us from Him?

1 Timothy 6:9–10 says, "People who want to get rich fall into temptation and a trap and into many foolish and harmful desires that plunge men into ruin and destruction. For the love

of money is a root of all kinds of evil. Some people, eager for money, have wandered from the faith and pierced themselves with many grief's."

People can be very poor and still be victims.

How so?

They are poor and simply *want* to get rich. It is not *being* rich that is the problem; it is *wanting* to be rich. Money is not the problem; the *love* of money is the real issue.

Another misunderstanding is that, somehow, money is *the* root of *all* evil. Read 1 Timothy again. The love of money is *a* root of *all sorts* of evil, not *the* root. It is like one of many roots belonging to a huge oak tree. The tree has many roots that keep it upright. Evil has many roots keeping it alive, not just the love of money. There are many ways to be evil that don't involve money.

Money isn't evil; Satan is.

The ultimate concern should be the heart of the person managing the money. A wrong motive or attitude toward money can lead to all sorts of problems. One such problem is greed.

Let's look at Luke 12:13–21, The Parable of the Rich Fool.

[13] *Someone in the crowd said to him, "Teacher, tell my brother to divide the inheritance with me."*

[14] *Jesus replied, "Man, who appointed me a judge or an arbiter between you?"* [15] *Then He said to them, "Watch out! Be on your guard against all kinds of greed; life does not consist in an abundance of possessions."*

[16] *And He told them this parable: "The ground of a certain rich man yielded an abundant harvest.* [17] *He thought to himself, 'What shall I do? I have no place to store my crops.'*

[18] *"Then he said, 'This is what I'll do. I will tear down my barns and build bigger ones, and there I will store my surplus grain.* [19] *And I'll*

say to myself, "You have plenty of grain laid up for many years. Take life easy; eat, drink and be merry."'

[20] *"But God said to him, 'You fool! This very night your life will be demanded from you. Then who will get what you have prepared for yourself?'*

[21] *"This is how it will be with whoever stores up things for themselves but is not rich toward God."*

Greed makes us do all sorts of bad things. People break rules to steal things from others. We often sacrifice time with our families for more money. We can become so focused on ourselves, on what we have, and on preparing for more that we lose sight of what is more important — our relationship with God.

Luke 12:13–21 tells us not to focus on having things because, when we die, they are gone. Instead, we should focus on the things that are of eternal value.

Gaining more for the sake of gaining more is pointless.

I'm sure you've been asked this before, but have you ever seen a U-Haul behind a hearse?

Your life could come to an end today.

And if it did, what would you have?

Nothing, if you were not rich in God.

When it comes to investing, greed will cause you to do things you would not otherwise do. Making money requires good decisions. If those decisions become effected by greed, you'll make mistakes that can be very costly.

How can you know that greed is affecting you when it comes to investing?

Without rules, it can be hard to know if greed is present. Rules create guidelines to operate by, thereby defeating greed. If these rules aren't followed, it is usually a sign of wanting more when you shouldn't be.

It is difficult to sell something that has made you money. You want it to make you more. If what you want overcomes the obedience to follow rules, greed has set in. Deciding to follow rules, prior to actually needing them, removes the emotion most people encounter at the time the decision needs to be made. Make the rules based on what is the right thing to do.

Rules trump greed.

You could simply not have rules, and then you would never break any.

Nice try!

But that would mean you are flying blind and sure to crash.

KEY NUMBER THREE: Rich in God

The source of man's contentment was designed by our creator to come only from Him.

Matthew 6:33 says, "But seek first His kingdom and His righteousness, and all these things will be given to you as well."

And Matthew 22:37–38 says, "Jesus replied: 'Love the Lord your God with all your heart and with all your soul and with all your mind.' This is the first and greatest commandment."

If we will do these things, God will keep our hearts close to Him and not allow us to fall in love with anything else.

How many people do you know who have money and things and still are not satisfied?

They model the Howard Hughes answer, always thinking they need "just a little bit more."

Billy Graham says, "There is nothing wrong with people possessing riches. The wrong comes when riches possess people."

Why can't we seek our contentment from being obedient to God?

We should find joy in having a great relationship with Him and trusting that He will take care of us. As we gain more money and possessions through the progression of life, we should be willing to give to the church and toward the needs of others, as we have the ability to do so, thereby demonstrating that our hearts are right with God and that we can be obedient in tithing and helping others. If we don't do this, our hearts could become greedy and allow us to fall in love with money.

Dr. Charles Stanley pastors a church in Atlanta, Georgia, and has written many books. One that I love is titled, *How to Reach Your Full Potential for God.*

In the book, he says, "The stingy, greedy, sinful, lustful, wasteful person who is totally self-centered and self-gratifying does *not* experience quality of life at any age, much less old age. By comparison, a person who is joyful, generous, loving, kind, faithful, and peaceful can, and often does, enjoy a tremendously high-quality life—even without many material possessions, comforts, or luxuries."

Dr. Stanley also has a great principle he lives by. He splits his money up into thirds. One third of the money he receives is returned to God through tithes and offerings, another third is used for taking care of his immediate family and others, and the last third is used to enjoy life.

What a great way to live and stay in balance!

Gaining more money isn't the pitfall. Falling in love with a tool, money, is the real danger.

If you followed Charles Stanley's lead and divvied up your money into thirds, giving back to God's work, providing for your family and others, and enjoying life, could you really have too much money?

DEADLY TRAP NUMBER FOUR: Slave to Money

Luke 16:13 tells us, "No one can serve two masters. Either you will hate the one and love the other, or you will be devoted to the one and despise the other. You cannot serve both God and money."

Like many things in life that can be used as a tool, money has the potential to help us or harm us. If money is used for harmful purposes, such as buying illegal drugs, it can become a bad tool.

But is money itself bad?

How can the tool be bad?

A gun is harmless if left in a hidden compartment. A gun used to harvest a deer to feed a family becomes a great tool. A gun in an evil person's hand used to shoot another human being, maybe to steal their money and leave them for dead, is an example of a tool becoming harmful. Ultimately, it is the hand of the person who holds the tool that assigns its value.

Money is a tool. It can be used for good or for evil.

You probably have some tools in the garage or a utility room in your house. Growing up, I saw many tools that my dad had in various places. Some hung up on the walls in the garage, others were found in a toolbox, and others he had in the house in drawers in strategic places.

Tools can be used to help us accomplish many things. Money can be a great tool.

But can a tool become a master?

Well, here are some things I've noticed about tools: We often buy tools to do a job that others could have done for us because we realize that having the tool and doing the job ourselves saves us money, plus the tool will remain with us for a long time. If the need arises again for the same tool, we'll have it handy to use, thereby saving us money again.

So if we perceive value in it, we'll likely buy a tool. We'll use the tool for the immediate job at hand (which also requires our time). Then we'll put the tool away, hopefully where it can be readily found for the next job.

As the tool becomes used, we discover that maintenance of the tool is required. An axe requires sharpening. A circular saw requires a new blade or, at least, sharpening. Maintenance requires our time, and maybe additional money, to keep the tools prepared for their next use.

We also find ourselves rearranging, organizing, and moving our tools. If we change locations, those tools get carted along and find a new home as well. These money-saving tools can begin to enslave us to a lifetime of service to them. We can become consumed with searching for, purchasing, using, maintaining, storing, and managing our tools.

At what point does money, a tool, become a master?

If the attainment of money becomes what consumes you, and you can never have enough of it, then it has mastered you. You will do whatever is required to keep it and to get more of it. The desire to be rich, the love of money, and the compulsion of greed spring to life, and your heart assigns improper value to money. Your values get scrambled, and soon, the entire reason you live is for money. Money could then reach idol status, completely replacing God in your life. If you develop a vision that lots of money will take care of you, then you could be fooled into believing that money can replace God.

If this happens, money has become your master. You have chosen to work for, or serve, money instead of making it work for you.

You cannot serve two masters.

The good steward manages money, understanding that it is simply a tool. Regardless of how much money the steward manages, the money remains servant to the steward. The good and faithful servant remains true to his master, God.

To be the good and faithful servant, you'll need to avoid the number one deadly trap of remaining in fear. You'll need to realize that you will encounter fear, but you must not remain in its presence.

If a man who is unfamiliar with street crossing stands at a busy crosswalk, frozen in fear, for a few minutes, there's no problem. If he is still standing there days later, there is a big problem.

Gaining knowledge and wisdom will lead to having faith and taking action. You can escape fear by using the number one key you must possess — faith.

As you seek stewardship, you'll need to avoid the second deadly trap of having too much money. You can avoid the trap of too much money by being sure that you possess key number two, a generous heart, allowing you to give back to God and help others. This will also aid in avoiding the next trap.

Deadly trap number three is greed and falling in love with money. Being a steward of money requires you to have rules you follow and to pursue loving God, which will prevent you from loving the wrong things, one of which is money.

Key number three that you must possess is the desire to be rich in God. You can do this by following the greatest commandment, which Matthew 22:37–38 tells us is to love God with all your heart, soul, and mind.

Will you fall victim to deadly trap number four and become a slave to money, always working for a little bit more because you love and serve money, or will you serve God and always work toward becoming the good and faithful servant?

If you can avoid the four deadly traps and grab hold of the three keys, you'll be racing down the road that leads to becoming a great steward and hearing, "Well done, my good and faithful servant."

God's Fingerprint

"See there's this place in me where your fingerprints still rest, your kisses still linger, and your whispers softly echo. It's the place where a part of you will forever be a part of me."

~Gretchen Kemp

One day, as I was about to leave for work, I heard the piano chiming away. My daughter, Ava, was five years old at the time and was learning to play.

When I walked into the room, she quickly pointed out that she was trying to learn how to play a song from memory. I was impressed with her ambition. She, on the other hand, was clearly frustrated.

In the blink of an eye, the thought raced through my mind: *Why wouldn't the Decision-Maker DNA work here too?*

Remembering how I had learned of the *Decision-Maker DNA* while reading about Peter in Acts, chapter 10, I knew the process well.

I told Ava to do the following:

1. Play the song all the way through, using the book.
2. Close the book.
3. Think about the song for a minute.

Then I said, "Repeat this process **three times**. After the third time, leave the book closed, and play the song."

I gave her a hug and left for work.

When I returned home that evening and walked in the door, Ava came running as hard as she could.

She threw her arms around me and gave me a big squeeze, yelling, "Dad! Dad! It worked! It worked!"

I stood there, thinking, for a second: *What is she talking about?*

Then it hit me.

"You played the song from memory, didn't you?"

"Yes! It worked! It worked!"

Talk about being a hero! Superman had nothing on me that day.

Ava had learned to play a song from memory using the *Decision-Maker DNA*, which says that we will understand, accept, or believe after **three repetitions**.

A few months later, our son, Wyatt, who was just a few months short of two years old, was playing with some wooden blocks on the floor. It was Awana night (a program for children) at our church, and Mom and Ava were there until later in the evening. This was the time that Wyatt and I had together, once a week, to do whatever two guys wanted to do.

As I lay there on the floor, building small towers and watching Wyatt tear them down before they reached monumental size, I wondered about Wyatt and his ability to count. Mom had been working with him, to some degree, on counting and recognizing numbers, so I decided it was time for another experiment.

I took four blocks and lined them up in a row. I pointed to each as I counted them, one by one, and then asked Wyatt if he could do the same thing.

He pointed to each block and quickly uttered some numbers, like, "One…three…seven…nine."

I repeated this exercise, once again demonstrating how to count each block.

Again, Wyatt made an attempt that went something like, "One…two…five…seven."

(I'm sure you know where this is going.)

Once more, I counted each block as I pointed to it.

Wyatt had watched me count the blocks *three times* now, and his third attempt was at hand.

Would he do it?

Even though I believed in the value of repeating **three times**, I really was not expecting him to do it. I guess that my faith in what had appeared to be true was not quite there yet.

Slowly and methodically, as though it was second nature and really easy to do, Wyatt pointed to each block.

"One…two…three…four."

I couldn't believe it!

As I came to understand the power in the third occurrence, I couldn't help but ask myself:

Why three?

Why was three the number of repetitions needed to help us understand, accept, or believe?

Why not two?

Why wasn't four the number...or even five?

Scripture would reveal the answer.

Matthew 28:19 says, "Therefore go and make disciples of all nations, baptizing them in the name of the Father and of the Son and of the Holy Spirit,"

Three is the number representing God Himself.

He exists as **three beings**:

1.   The Father
2.   The Son
3.   The Holy Spirit

All combined to make one complete God — **three in one**.

In scripture, God is often described as:

1.   The God of Abraham
2.   The God of Isaac
3.   The God of Jacob

His name is **three letters**:

1.   G
2.   O
3.   D

The number three began to jump out of the Bible, yelling and screaming, begging me to look.

Knowing that my ninety-year-old grandmother reads the Bible all the time, I mentioned this to her. She, too, began to see the threes. She found it unbelievable that she had never noticed it before. And she has read the Bible more than any other single person I know. Our conversations had always included the Bible, God, and creation. But from then on, they would also include our latest discoveries on the number three.

What came next simply amazed me.

As you read this, even though your eyes are open, try to visualize this as you go. Think about the fact that some people believe the Bible isn't real and God didn't create everything around us, including each one of us. And then, for a minute, think about the probability of all the threes you are about to witness just appearing by chance.

Is it possible that a large number of men, over a long period of time, could record so many threes into the Bible by chance and not by God's design?

I don't believe that for one second. And I'll bet that you won't either.

This is not a complete list of all the threes in the Bible; of that I'm sure. It is, however, a portion that creates a magnificent picture.

Imagine space — nothing but blackness.

In 2 Peter 3:5-6, we are reminded that everything was made from water.

Water requires **three elements**: two hydrogen plus one oxygen.

In the first chapter of Genesis, God creates everything.

Genesis 1:1 tells us, "In the beginning, God created the heavens and the earth."

Heavens is plural because **there are three**.

Paul mentions the third heaven in 2 Corinthians 12:2.

1. The first heaven includes our planet and its atmosphere.

2. The second heaven includes the planets, stars, and everything we can see outside of our atmosphere.

3. The third heaven is the final destination — where God is.

On **day three**, God brings the earth into existence.

He then places the sun and moon for our light during the day and night, totaling **three celestial bodies** that are essential to our existence:

1. The earth
2. The sun
3. The moon

Where did the earth end up being?

It is the **third planet** from the sun.

On day six, everything was finished, and Genesis 1:31 says, "God saw all that He had made, and it was very good."

There are many threes in the Old Testament.

Here are a few more:

In Genesis 6 and 7, before the great flood, Noah and his **three sons** build the ark.

In Genesis 8, Noah discovers when the flood is over by sending out a dove **three times**.

In Daniel, chapter 6 describes the reason for Daniel going into the lion's den.

What was the reason?

He was praying **three times** a day.

In Jonah 1, we learn that Jonah lives in the belly of a whale for **three days and nights**.

In Daniel 3, **three men**—Shadrach, Meshach, and Abednego—are thrown into the fiery furnace for their refusal to worship the king.

Some New Testament threes are even more powerful.

Starting with and focusing mainly on Christ Himself:

In Matthew 2, Jesus is born. **Three magi** – more commonly known as the **three wise men or kings** – bring gifts to Jesus.[2]

In Luke 2, at the age of twelve, Christ is separated from his parents, and it takes them **three days** to find him.

In Luke 3:23, at the **age of thirty**, Christ begins His ministry, which would last for **three years** (based on timed events in Scripture).

In Luke 4, Satan tempts Christ **three times** and then gives up.

Jesus **raises three** from the dead: the widow's son in Luke 7:11–17, Jarius's daughter in Luke 8:54–55, and Lazarus in John 11:33–34.

In Mark 14, Jesus prays in Gethsemane **three times** before He goes to the cross.

In Luke 23, Pilate attempts **three times** to persuade the people to let Jesus go.

In Mark 15, Christ (at **thirty-three years** of age) is put on one of **three crosses**. He is placed on the cross on the **third hour** (9:00 a.m. Roman time). He will remain there for **three hours** before the sun is darkened. After another **three hours**, at **3:00 p.m.**, He dies.

In Mark 8, after being buried, Christ rises on the **third day**.

John 3, verses 16 and 17, explains why all this occurs.

Where do you go after your life here on Earth ends?

If you believe John 3:16, you go to the **third heaven**, where God is, forever.

Luke 24:6–7 says that the gospel needs **three events** to be complete:

1. Death
2. Burial
3. Resurrection

John 14:6 tells us that Christ is **three things** to us:

1. The way
2. The truth
3. The life

What about this great country?

Looking at the United States of America, we'll also see God's mark in several places. (And American historians, I'm sure, will think of other significant threes as well.)

When the English colonists first came to Virginia in 1607, **three ships** carried them across the ocean:

1. The *Susan Constant*
2. The *Godspeed*
3. The *Discovery*

Three great documents created the foundation for this country:

1. The Declaration of Independence
2. The Constitution
3. The Bill of Rights

Our Declaration of Independence promises the people **three things**:

1. Life
2. Liberty
3. The Pursuit of Happiness

The workings of our government exist as **three separate branches**:

1. The executive
2. The legislative
3. The judicial

These branches create a system of checks and balances—a brilliant design and one that I believe to be ordained by God.

What about our flag?

Even though it has undergone some changes since the beginning, it has **three colors** that it proudly displays:

1. Red
2. White
3. Blue

Could this be an accident?

Not a chance!

If you wanted to abbreviate the United States of America, how would you do it?

I bet it would be with **three letters**:

1. U
2. S
3. A

When God created man, or human beings, He also used a few markers.

According to 1 Thessalonians 5:23, man consists of **three separate parts**:

1. Spirit
2. Soul
3. Body

One of our most essential attributes is sight. Without our eyes, we would hardly have a chance of surviving on our own.

But have you thought about how your eyes work?

There are millions of cone cells in each eye, which are responsible for color vision. In order for us to see a continuous range of colors, we have **three types** of cone cells that work together.

The colors we see all originate from **three primary colors** of light:

1. Red
2. Blue
3. Green

The primary colors are mixed to make up all the colors we see.

What about our brains?

The average adult brain weighs about **three pounds** and has **three main parts**:

1. The cerebrum
2. The cerebellum
3. The brain stem

Really! I'm not making this up.

The human body is a tremendous creation.

The oxygen, organic compounds, and energy needed for all life on Earth come from photosynthesis.

For photosynthesis to occur, **three things** are needed:

1. Sunlight
2. Water
3. Carbon dioxide

Even the basis for everything in the universe starts with atoms, which are made up of **three parts**:

1. Protons
2. Neutrons
3. Electrons

The basic existence of everything is defined by **three sets of three**:

1. Form — gas, liquid, and solid
2. Shape — height, width, and depth
3. Time — past, present, and future

There are only **three things** that we can spend:

1. Time
2. Energy
3. Money

There are only **three ways** by which we can travel:

1. Land
2. Sea
3. Air

And I'm sure you've heard one of the expressions, "**third time** lucky" or "**third time's** a charm."

I love the fact that God clearly used the number three to mark events throughout the Bible, our country, and ourselves, as if to say, "That was me!"

Because God exists as three, He left His fingerprint, the number three, on us and a lot of the world in which we live. I hope this helps you to understand why the number three is so powerful.

Now you know why:

Three is the fingerprint of God.

My Moses Journey

"Blessed are all who fear the Lord, who walk in obedience to him."

~Psalm 128:1

In the Introduction of this book, I mentioned that I would share my mistakes. This was, by far, the hardest chapter to write. I wanted to include it, so you could witness my journey and the hard-won lessons that I hope will be an encouragement to you. These are not lessons directly concerning the stock market. They are lessons on living life and how important our trust, faith, and obedience to God really are.

You are reading this book for one reason:

In spite of all my delays, doubts, and poor excuses, I'm being obedient to God.

I believe we all have a Moses journey in some way.

Like Moses and others in the Bible, I thought that God had chosen poorly in selecting me for this mission. I had a whole bunch of reasons to justify this false belief about myself.

In sharing my personal journey, it is my goal that you will see how God has worked in my life as well as my trials and struggles to bring myself into alignment with His vision for my life.

Here we go!

It was a terrific day, graduating cum laude from Ohio University in 1989. My first four-and-a-half years of independence had landed me with both a Bachelor of Business Administration degree, and a degree in management information systems.

Later that summer, I accepted my first job with Columbia Gas of Ohio, in their computer programming department, making more money than I ever thought a twenty-three-year-old could.

At that point, I began to learn how valuable money really was. I had accumulated around fifteen thousand dollars of debt in student loans. Almost five years of college had forced me to borrow from a local bank and work while in school. When I absolutely had to, I borrowed from my dad just to get by.

Working all day every day for a paycheck, money took on new meaning. What an eye opener that was!

After a year or so, having managed to save a few thousand dollars, I recalled a college class in which I had been introduced to the topic of investing. It was during my junior year. A substitute teacher had diverged from the class syllabus for *three weeks* and taught us about the stock market using a book titled, *How to Buy Stocks,* by Louis Engel and Brenden Boyd.

I thought: *That's it! I need to invest the few thousand dollars I have and let them make more for me.*

Little did I know, that thought and the actions that followed would change my life dramatically.

In 1990, I opened an investment account with about three thousand dollars. Studying William O'Neil's book, *How to Make Money in Stocks,* and using his Daily Graphs service, which my brother had discovered in the library, I began making a little money as I learned a lot about a whole new world — and about myself.

Over the next three to four years, my imagination of the possibilities in the stock market outgrew the day-to-day task of sitting behind a desk, searching for problems buried in seventeen thousand lines of computer code. William O'Neil's success, described in his book, made me realize there was more to life than getting up every day knowing what my pay would be, regardless of how smart or how hard I worked.

When three thousand dollars grew to over fifteen thousand by the end of 1993, I knew I was on the right track.

In May of 1994, I married my beloved wife, Sheryl, and our dreams were around every corner. We had met at Columbia Gas, where she, too, had worked as a computer programmer.

Later that year, my stock market experience was telling me I could do better if only I had more time. The additional time would allow me to do better research, and I would be able to monitor prices in real time. Investing full time became a real ambition and consideration.

In early 1995, during a workday lunch break, I drove a few minutes down the road to the Kroger supermarket to get a salad for lunch. I remember it well because that was the day that the thought of investing full time became a reality. As I ate my lunch in the truck, listening to the radio, a voice came across the airwaves (the airwaves only I could hear).

I'm sure it was the voice of God, whispering, "It's all right."

I remember thinking: *Was that you, God?*

I couldn't believe it!

Just moments earlier, I had thought about wanting to end my computer job and invest money for a living. The thought of quitting my job was both exciting and scary. I would only make money if I could invest well.

Even with God's assurance, I couldn't help but think: *How could this be right?*

I had spent the last five-and-a-half years working at a job with great pay, good benefits, and paid vacation. Before that, I had spent four-and-a-half years in college, going into debt by way of student loans and working hard to graduate with honors. I had invested ten years of my life into this job.

Now, I'm considering walking away and going in a completely different direction?

Fortunately for me, my dad had cancelled my debt with him. It was his way of rewarding me for making it through college with flying colors. Unfortunately, the bank debt stayed with me. But I was sure that God had just given me the thumbs up, sitting right there in the Kroger parking lot.

Now, the big question was: *What would my wife of less than a year think?*

As we sat in the back room of our little rental house one night and discussed what it would take for me to start investing full time and for us to live on only Sheryl's salary, we wrote down all of our expenses and added them up. Sheryl's take-home pay was equal to our expenses minus what we normally spent on birthday presents and Christmas.

Ouch!

This new job wasn't sounding so rosy.

But the fire behind me was burning much hotter, and a few numbers couldn't cool me down. Besides, God had given me the go-ahead, and He knew our situation. Still, as I sat looking at the list of our yearly outflows, my eye caught one category that had the potential to make a big difference if we simply stopped.

What would you guess it to be?

Shamefully, it was our tithe. I remember looking at Sheryl.

The look on her face said, "Don't even go there," and we committed to remain faithful.

We both agreed:

There was no way that we were going to stop tithing or even cheat a little, even if it meant we had to cut back somewhere else where it would hurt.

I'm glad we made a good decision and remained obedient. Although I can't prove it, I firmly believe that, had we not honored God with our tithe at that point in time, the future would not have developed as it did.

In July of 1995, it was a surreal moment as my brother, Dave, and I sat down together in the back room of his house. Dave had been investing full time for about nine months, and until now, our communication had been limited to lunch times. It was exciting, getting up every day, anticipating great things, and being free to make decisions that would have a direct impact on our future.

From here on out, we were both full-time investors. I still remember the excitement of those first few years. From 1995 to 1998, I made some and lost some, but overall, I made good progress. I learned a lot about my opinion, how it was interfering with my results, and how very important the overall stock market and its direction were.

I also learned that I had the ability to spot a winner at the right time. I just needed to pull it all together. I believe I started near seventeen or eighteen thousand dollars in 1995. That money had grown from about three thousand in 1991. The big opportunity came in the fall of 1998. Sheryl and I had added some additional money to our stock account, providing around forty thousand to start 1998.

Later that year, the markets were tanking hard. It was the perfect storm, and all the hard work was coming full circle. Dave and I worked as a team and performed together like a well-oiled machine. The value of the skills I had acquired — understanding the market's health and direction, finding leading stocks among thousands, buying them at exactly the right time, and using leverage, when appropriate — paid off massively. Sheryl and I were amazed as our forty thousand dollars grew to over two million in about one-and-a-half years.

We even won a contest, held by *Investor's Business Daily*, for the best performance over the three-year period of 1998–2000.

Investor's Business Daily also featured us in the "Smart Investor" section of the paper, where they reported that I had managed to gain a jaw-dropping 3,400 percent, and Dave had gained over 1,800 percent. (My gains were actually 5,000 percent, but they omitted almost five hundred thousand dollars in withdrawals that had I made from my account during their calculations.)

It was almost too good to be true. But it *was* true. Life was grand.

We were on cloud twenty-five, and heaven was just a cloud away. I only wish that someone had warned me about clouds. They don't have floors.

In 1999, we bought our first house, and the following year, we purchased a large piece of real estate. We were really optimistic about our future. The big piece of real estate became known as the Four-Hundred-Acre Wood. It is a beautiful place in the rolling hills of Ohio, with forest and large, open fields.

Later, we built a dam, creating a five-acre lake in the middle of it, without a house in sight for nearly a mile in any direction. The only man-made sound you hear when you visit the Four-Hundred-Acre Wood is the occasional jet flying overhead or the click-clack echo of horses' hooves as they pull an Amish-drawn buggy on the distant road.

The views from the hilltops can keep you captivated for hours, leaving you wishing you could stay forever. The Four-Hundred-Acre Wood was definitely a godsend and is a story in itself. We are now planning to build our family's home there.

In 2000, Sheryl left her full-time job to become a full-time mom, an even bigger job but one that didn't pay the bills or help reduce our debt. We didn't have children yet, but we were praying for them to come soon and expand our lives.

What I didn't know was that the market was about to decline in a way very similar to the October 1929 crash, which created a bear market lasting until 1932. This period of market devastation was duplicated from 2000 to 2003, some of the hardest and most challenging years during which one could ever have been involved with the stock market.

How badly I wish I'd had a mentor to keep me grounded and prepared for those tough years.

During this time, I engaged the market according to the rules I had used just years earlier, only to be chased away each time, losing up to 8 or 10 percent. Losses and bills were taking their toll. Every time we paid bills, the tool I used to make a living— money—was steadily disappearing. I was bleeding money everywhere.

We only had two debts, but they were big ones—our house and the Four-Hundred-Acre Wood. We also had to write the IRS income tax checks for almost one million dollars because of our success. (I am not complaining. I love this country and the opportunity it affords me and my family.) Buying our house or the property weren't the mistakes.

I made two mistakes all by myself:

1. I allowed too much debt—slavery-type debt. I should have made larger down payments on both of the large purchases or, even better, paid for them in full.

2. I failed to give a complete tithe, which is 10 percent. I gave what I thought was a lot.

Prior to quitting my job, we had tithed as we should have. But when the numbers got big and Uncle Sam got involved, giving 10 percent was hard to do. Obedience is a choice, a very important one. God doesn't ask us to give a lot, but He expects 10 percent, regardless of how big or small it appears to us.

I couldn't help but think about Moses and his big mistake. Nearing the end of his time in Egypt, he had killed an Egyptian in defense of one of his Hebrew brothers. I'm sure that, at the time, he had believed in what he was doing and that the people would realize he was going to help free them. But they didn't, and Pharaoh wanted his head. Moses fled to Midian to spend the next forty years in a desert.

I, too, was feeling the heat, and the desert was straight ahead.

From 2003 to 2006, there were small losses and an occasional big gain. The problem was that big gains on small amounts didn't go far. I was making 50 to 100 percent—sometimes 200 percent or more—only to barely survive. I had definitely learned to follow the "keep your losses small" rule. But small losses, big percentage gains on small amounts, and lots of bills equaled trouble. It was a time of struggle for our financial survival.

Our first child, Ava, arrived beautifully in 2003. She was the gem in the rough times we faced. As each day passed, every time we looked at her, we couldn't help but see how awesome God is. She gave Sheryl and me hope for the future. I believe that is part of the reason for her middle name, Grace.

After a few years passed, I had major back surgery in January of 2006, and then our handsome son, Wyatt, came along a few months later. It was amazing to see God bring the excitement of more life to our home at such a financially dismal time. Wyatt was, from the beginning, and is, presently, a strong young man.

His middle name, Samuel, fits him well and is exactly what our house needed — strength dedicated to the Lord.

Those years were bitter and sweet. Money was vaporizing, and I was scrambling. I knew that if something didn't change, life would become very troublesome. The pressure was on.

Hudson Taylor once wrote, "It doesn't matter how great the pressure is; what really matters is where the pressure lies. Whether it comes between you and God or presses you nearer His heart."

In 2006, something miraculous happened. God allowed me to see the foundation of what I now call the *Triple Tank System.* (You read about the aha moment in the chapter titled, *Could Warren Buffett be Wrong?*)

I couldn't stop thinking about it.

But I did ask God one question, "Will you please prove it to me?"

To use this newly gained wisdom, I needed to fully understand the realness of it, and I needed more proof and evidence. After all, if I was going to associate God with an investment system, it needed to be rock solid.

Over time, it became more than that. It was almost unbelievable. I kept researching over the next three years.

By 2009, I had found all kinds of evidence in the Bible to support why it worked as it did. I had proved that it was an ongoing event by finding many occurrences of it in the markets. Even more research revealed that the markets had been acting this way all the way back to the 1890s — the earliest stock market information I could find. The pattern and the mechanics could be quantified, and a system could be developed.

God was definitely proving what He had shown me years before.

An overwhelming sense of responsibility hit me like a ton of bricks. I couldn't imagine my time on this earth ending without a chance to share this with Ava and Wyatt. But because they were too young to understand it now, I needed to write everything down for them.

I called a great friend of mine, Troy, who is an English teacher, and talked his ear off for hours that night about this God-given discovery, writing it down, and teaching it to others. After talking with Troy, I sat up thinking about the fact that I knew nothing about how to assemble this information in a way that I could later use to teach my kids.

As I sat in silence, praying for guidance, I heard God clearly say, "Ron, if this is good enough for *your* children, it's good enough for *all* of my children."

Can you imagine how I responded?

I jumped for joy!

I was so excited about the possibility of sharing this with others.

Well, that wasn't quite how I responded.

My real response was, "Oh no, God, surely you don't mean you want me to share this with others. You're talking to someone who is about to lose his home. Besides, I can't speak to strangers about this. I'm not even a speaker. It just doesn't make sense."

I know it was silly, telling God something as if He didn't know. God knows I never planned on being an author, teacher, or public speaker. Those would have been numbers 101, 102, and 103 on my list of 100 things I wanted to do.

Again, Moses came to mind. God humbled Moses and taught him to be a servant during his mid-years of life in the desert. At eighty years of age (in Exodus, chapters 3 and 4), Moses provided two excuses to God for why he couldn't lead the people out of Egypt.

On his third and final attempt to persuade God, Moses practically begged, saying, "Pardon your servant, Lord. Please send someone else."

I was thinking the exact same thing. I only wanted to be sure that my kids would have this newly gained insight into the financial markets, not to go on a mission—especially one that I didn't feel qualified to go on and that would require time and money, neither of which were in abundance.

It can often be one of the most difficult things in the world to do, to follow God's direction when you can't understand why or how. It is at those times that your faith is revealed.

Will you let something come between you and God?

Or will you draw nearer to His heart?

The only way I could think of to share this system with the rest of the world was to write a book, so I began researching and learning how to do that by attending a workshop taught by Steve Harrison. It was an eye-opening experience, and it taught me many valuable lessons on writing and what is required if you want to help others. I also learned from Tim Paulson that we all have a title that describes who we are—in this case, a title to a book.

During this time, my pastor asked me if I would teach Sunday school. I said yes, having no clue that this, too, was part of God's bigger vision for my life.

God has a great way of preparing us for the future that He has planned for us.

I wasn't broke, but I was cash poor. My mom was instrumental in providing the resources I needed; she believed this difficult time would pass.

Isn't it wonderful to have family members who believe in you?

Just months earlier, our home had been sold in foreclosure.

By late 2010, I had been teaching Sunday school for a while, and I enjoyed it. Speaking to a small group was actually a lot of fun, especially since the subject matter was what I love. I also started tiptoeing into the new system, *The Triple Tank*. Over time, the system was fully developed and rules were created.

My biggest challenge wasn't believing in the system God had shown me, it was getting past the idea of using something new. But I discovered that it could, and should, be used in conjunction with what I had learned many years ago from William O'Neil; it didn't have to be used in place of what I already knew. It was a great new tool—a new system that almost never failed, eliminated risk, and maximized gains. It provided more certainty than I had ever seen for starting a position in an index or stock.

It was also in 2010 that I signed an oil and gas lease on a large portion of the Four-Hundred-Acre Wood that we had bought in 2000.

Just a year after we had bought the land, I was walking on it and stopped to look over a beautiful spot when God shared with me a confounding truth.

"Ron, as long as you own this land, it will take care of you."

At the time, it didn't make sense to me at all. It only began to make sense in 2010 when I signed the oil and gas lease. We got a check for signing the lease, and it was a big mistake. When I signed the lease, I ignored more recent guidance. It was God's warning, which came in the form of what we sometimes describe as that little voice we hear.

The message was clear: "Don't sign the lease."

I didn't understand.

Why shouldn't I accept money right now?

It was much needed. It didn't make sense not to sign.

What did I do?

I ignored God's warning and leased the property.

The timing was not right, and God knew what I had no way of knowing: that the land was worth a lot more than what I was being offered.

The money helped a little. My disobedience hurt a lot.

When 2011 turned into the end of 2012 — in spite of my mistake and through God's grace — I was given an opportunity to amend the oil and gas lease and *was paid fifty times more* than what I had received in 2010.

Our mistakes aren't big enough that God can't fix them.

In 2014, I discovered the full benefit of God's promise when an oil company informed me of the possible future value of my land. Listening to this news reminded me of His promise that, as long as I owned the land, it would take care of me.

It now appears that God over-delivered by a hundred times or more than anything I could have imagined that promise to mean. Simply amazing!

His promise has, indeed, come full circle. The land was, and is still becoming, a huge blessing to my family and me.

God certainly proved this system to me, and I knew it could be relied upon. Even so, I have struggled to write this book, the strategy guide, and model book to teach you this system. I've started and stopped more times than I like to admit. My lack of faith in my ability to write what I knew to be true conflicted with my own personal situation. Self-doubt and lack of understanding kept me wondering, much like Moses did, why God had chosen me.

When I was young, I remember watching the movie, *The Ten Commandments*, starring Charlton Heston. I loved the scene in which the Red Sea parted, and everyone passed through. It's hard to imagine being there and walking the dry ground between two great walls of water.

What a sight!

Sometimes, in life, we run into our own Red Sea that appears to have us trapped. There is no way to go around, and there doesn't seem to be a way through.

But we know this isn't true.

Matthew 19:26 says, "with man this is impossible, but with God, all things are possible."

Please don't misunderstand me.

I'm not claiming to be Moses — *not even close.*

But I do know that events in my life resemble his in many ways. This can be one of the many benefits of studying the Bible. God can show us others who have made mistakes and have still gone on to do great things with Him at their sides.

Had I studied the life of Moses earlier in my life, would I have made the same decisions?

From whose life in the Bible can you learn and benefit?

What mistakes can you avoid?

And if you've made mistakes, don't panic. So did Moses. So have I.

God doesn't use perfect people to do great things. He uses those willing to do something with Him, *so that all people will know how great He is.*

Dwight L. Moody once commented on Moses, saying, "He

spent his first forty years thinking he was somebody. He spent his second forty years learning he was a nobody. He spent his third forty years discovering what God can do with a nobody."

God helped me through my own Red Sea, one I created by mistakes and my own disobedience. As I walk with Him toward the Promised Land, I don't know how the rest of the journey goes. Nobody does. But there is one thing I know for sure. God is with me.

And who knows?

Maybe you will be too.

Moses didn't part the Red Sea. He led the people through it to the other side.

My goal isn't to steer you around Wall Street. It's to lead you through it and then to hear, "Well done, my good and faithful servant."

The Ten Commandments of the Successful Investor™

"But blessed is the one who trusts in the Lord, whose confidence is in him. They will be like a tree planted by the water that sends out its roots by the stream. It does not fear when heat comes; its leaves are always green. It has no worries in a year of drought and never fails to bear fruit."

~Jeremiah 17:7–8

God carved the Ten Commandments into stone. Moses presented them to the people to be a permanent record of how we should live our daily lives. If we ignore them, we do so at our own peril.

The Ten Commandments presented here are my personal rules for investing. If you allow them to, I believe they will also guide you in becoming a successful investor and a great steward.

***

ONE: Thou Shall Seek God's Wisdom

Matthew 6:33 says, "But seek first His kingdom and His righteousness, and all these things will be given to you as well."

One of the best things you can do is to seek God and His wisdom. The fulfillment of life's needs and the answers to your most difficult and challenging problems — all of these come to you when you keep the pursuit of God first.

Keep first things first.

TWO: Thou Shall Avoid Slavery

Luke 16:13 tells us that we cannot serve both God and money.

Money cannot be your master. If you allow yourself to owe money for things you possess, then your possessions own you. You work for them. You become their slave.

Your decisions will be influenced by your constant need for more money. What appears to be reasonable debt can become overpowering. Pressure will build, and bad decisions will follow.

A good steward will not allow himself to become a slave to debt. I broke this one, and it brought many tears.

THREE: Thou Shall Never, Never, Never Give Up

Matthew 19:26 tells us, "with God, all things are possible."

Becoming a good steward requires more than wanting to be one. It requires determination.

You must believe this thought: *I can do it. Failure is not an option.*

It must be solidly in your mind, cast in stone.

FOUR: Thou Shall Use a Proven System

John 14:6 says, "I am the way and the truth and the life. No one comes to the Father except through me."

If you want to go to heaven, there is but one way. The stock market is not the place to experiment. You must be sure that the system will produce the results you seek.

A good steward uses a proven system.

Henry Ford didn't reinvent the wheel, but he sure did put it to good use.

FIVE: Thou Shall Honor the System

Deuteronomy 5:16 says, "Honor your father and your mother, so that you may live long in the land the Lord your God is giving you."

I recommend honoring the method you use in the stock market for a similar reason, so that you may live long in the investment world. When you're tempted to change the method or to do something differently, make certain the changes are worthy.

Don't change what doesn't need changing.

SIX: Thou Shall Avoid the Most Deadly Three

Luke 12:15 says, "Then He said to them, 'Watch out! Be on your guard against all kinds of greed; life does not consist in an abundance of possessions.'"

Proverbs 16:18 says, "Pride goes before destruction, a haughty spirit before a fall."

Haggai 2:5 says, "This is what I covenanted with you when you came out of Egypt. And my Spirit remains among you. Do not fear."

Greed, pride, and fear will almost certainly destroy the efforts you make to become a good steward and invest well. Greed will make you break rules. Pride will make you argue. Fear will keep you frozen, unwilling to make the effort or a needed decision.

SEVEN: Thou Shall Cut Losses Quickly

Matthew 10:14 says, "If anyone will not welcome you or listen to your words, leave that home or town and shake the dust off your feet."

If what you've been doing isn't working, don't waste time waiting for things to change. Take action. In the market, the only thing you can do is to sell, thereby cutting your losses.

Then, stop and review the first six commandments.

EIGHT: Thou Shall Not Worry

Matthew 6:34 says, "Therefore do not worry about tomorrow, for tomorrow will worry about itself. Each day has enough trouble of its own."

You cannot worry about what might happen the next day or about whether you're right or wrong. Being a good steward and investing well requires you to make decisions. If you can make good decisions and act, then there is no need for worry.

Following the first seven commandments makes this much easier.

NINE: Thou Shall Listen

Genesis 42:21 says, "They said to one another, 'Surely we are being punished because of our brother. We saw how distressed he was when he pleaded with us for his life, but we would not listen; that's why this distress has come on us.'"

Refusing to listen often has bad consequences. Not listening to—or arguing with—the stock market can, and often will, have devastating results on your efforts toward being a good steward.

If you find yourself arguing with the market, then it's likely you're not listening.

TEN: Thou Shall Give Back

Malachi 3:10 says, "'Bring the whole tithe into the storehouse, that there may be food in my house. Test me in this,' says the Lord Almighty, 'and see if I will not throw open the floodgates of heaven and pour out so much blessing that there will not be room enough to store it.'"

A good steward recognizes that God is the owner of everything. He is willing and glad to give at least 10 percent, a tithe, to God. If you don't, you're stealing.

What future does a thief have?

If you feel like you don't have enough to give from, review the first nine commandments. They make commandment number ten possible.

At one time, I failed here too. Don't do it!

***

I believe that every successful investor should have a set of rules and guidelines by which they learn to live. Even after twenty years of investing in the stock market, I still need a daily reminder of the most important rules. I invite you to use them to your benefit.

Every time I ignored one of these rules, I paid a price.

Why make the same mistakes I did?

The Opportunity

"To succeed, jump as quickly at opportunities as you do at conclusions."

~Benjamin Franklin

While I can't guarantee that you'll be able to make 1,124 percent in seventeen days, I can promise you that there will be opportunities to make gains like those shown in the chapter titled, "Want Proof? *The Triple Tank.*"

Once you understand the advantage of *The Triple Tank* for getting the timing right and leveraging your money, exceptional gains will become possible. How I used *The Triple Tank* and the strategy to leverage the gain to 1,124 percent are covered in the *Triple Tank System* Strategy Guide.

The opportunities in the future will present themselves very similarly to some that you have seen in this book and others that you can see and study in the *Triple Tank System* Strategy Guide and Model Book.

If you prepare and are watchful, you'll have an opportunity to make percentage gains most believe are impossible. Others may think that it was luck, but you'll know differently. Plus, you'll be able to repeat it each time the opportunity presents itself in the future.

I've shared some of my life's biggest setbacks, my Moses moments. I'm sure that you've encountered some of your own.

But also, like Moses, I'm here to help you get to a better place. You might say that my goal is to lead you through a different Red Sea—one called Wall Street.

If you're young and are just getting started in life, maybe you haven't faced many disappointments yet. But as surely as the sun rises and sets, adversity will come. I spent some time on the mountaintop, fell nearly to my demise, and came back stronger than ever.

Charles Stanley once said, "Adversity is a setback from which we take our greatest leaps forward."

Regardless of your age, I know that you can make giant leaps forward.

In order to move forward, you will need to believe what I've shared in this book, learn to be patient and maintain your psychology, and be willing to learn the system, *The Triple Tank System*.

As Matthew chapter 25 points out so clearly, **Gods wants us to be investors**. Increasing our abilities is necessary if we want to become good stewards and have more to manage. It also tells us that *we must start now*. While we could go to a banker and deposit our money, earning whatever small amount of interest they'll pay, investing is the way to much bigger gains.

Robert Frost once said, "A bank is a place where they lend you an umbrella in fair weather and ask for it back when it begins to rain."

We can invest and gain more, or we can get scared, remain in fear, and hide what we have—eventually, keeping none. There really are only two choices: gain more, or keep none.

I'd rather be the investor, wouldn't you?

You've discovered your *Decision-Maker DNA* and how the Bible proves that we understand, accept, or believe after a third occurrence. This DNA represents itself in the stock market in the form of *The Triple Tank*.

Even though Warren Buffett says that we can't time the stock market in the short term, now you know that there is a method whereby we can know, with a very high level of certainty, that the stock market or a particular stock has reached bottom. This is when the future will begin to look brighter, and it's the time to put our money to work.

This is *not* bottom fishing. This is bottom *catching*.

Remember, the news will only serve to derail any chance you have at investing the right way. You must avoid selling when everyone on the planet is scared to death and avoid buying when the news sounds like Goldilocks just rode into town and will never leave.

If you'll learn a system, you'll be able to make good decisions based on what the market itself is telling you rather than on the news. You can learn to invest well by listening to the truth being told to you by the market itself, which is what real people are actually doing with real money.

As you gain skill and confidence and realize that the market isn't some undefeatable giant, you'll need to stay well-grounded. You'll need to avoid the four deadly traps of remaining in fear, too much money, greed and falling in love with money, and being a slave to money. You can defeat all four of these potentially deadly sins by possessing the three keys of faith, a generous heart, and a focus on becoming rich in God.

If you'll work on attaining and using these three keys while staying aware of the four deadly sins, you'll be certain to remain on the road that leads to becoming the good and faithful servant.

I hope that you'll refer quite often to the chapter titled, *The Ten Commandments of the Successful Investor*. God gave Moses the original Ten Commandments to help the people live lives that would be God-honoring and to keep them from committing sins that would separate them from God. The commandments I've included in this book are to help you live an investing life that will honor God and to help you prevent costly mistakes — ones that you really don't need to make.

I love what John Maxwell once said concerning mistakes and success.

He remarked, "It's said that a wise person learns from his mistakes. A wiser one learns from others' mistakes. But the wisest person of all learns from others' successes."

As you do well investing and strive to become the good and faithful servant, you must remember to keep money in its proper place, as a tool. As you gain more, you also need to focus not on becoming wealthy by the world's standards, but on seeking to become rich in God as you become a successful investor. As we witnessed in Matthew chapter 25, gaining more is a good thing. Our master expects us to do so.

I pray that this book has done at least three things:

1. Provided you with hope in moving forward and becoming a better steward of the money that God has entrusted to you.

2. Clearly shown you — in a way that you haven't seen before now — the wonderful and powerful God that we serve.

3. Caused you to clearly see the value in the *Decision-Maker DNA* and *The Triple Tank*, that they are the secret to eliminating risk and maximizing profits.

If you haven't already done so, the very best first step you can make is to invest your life in Christ. The final section of this book will help you to do that. Ultimately, it will be the very best investment you'll ever make — one that pays eternal dividends.

The second best thing you can do is to let me help you financially by teaching you how to use the *Decision-Maker DNA* and *The Triple Tank* in the financial markets. If there is one thing I wish someone had shared with me twenty years ago, it is this book and the *Triple Tank System* that I'm making available to you at:

www.RonTank.com

They will add to your abilities in becoming the good and faithful servant.

I'll show you actual history of how it has worked in the past, going all the way back to the 1890s. You'll also discover a system you can use to put *The Triple Tank* to work for you. The *Triple Tank System* will help you financially, and I hope that this book will benefit you just as much spiritually, which is far more valuable in the long run.

If you're concerned about learning and using the strategy guide and model book in the *Triple Tank System* program on your own, I completely understand.

When I was growing up, I remember the thought of soon being able to drive a car. I had several friends who loved to fish for largemouth bass as much as I did, and we couldn't get to our favorite fishing hole on our own yet, so the thought of driving brought pictures of being able to go fishing a lot.

But when I turned sixteen and was old enough to get a driving permit, a funny thing happened. I began to fear driving. The benefits of driving were being replaced by the idea of a scary event — me driving. I knew there would be many positives to driving besides being able to fish more often. But the positive aspect of driving was being beaten down by the thought of doing something I knew little about. I also understood that a mistake on the road could be devastating to me and my copilot.

The fear *almost* got the best of me. But the desire won, and I did learn to drive.

So what happened to cause the fear to take a back seat?

Fear was replaced by knowledge and wisdom, which were the keys to my willingness to try. Most of this knowledge was given to me on a trip with my dad, driving a 1976 four-speed Trans Am.

What a trip that was!

Riding along as he drove and explained about shifting, braking before turns, and accelerating through the turns, **what confidence I gained!**

Because I had experienced my dad's driving and knew he could drive well enough to compete in NASCAR, I trusted his advice and quickly believed I could do it. The knowledge I received was good. It wasn't my dad's opinion on how to drive; it was proven knowledge and wisdom used to drive a car.

Before I knew it, I was sitting behind the wheel of the Trans Am and driving it. My dad was the copilot, and I was as nervous as a big, fat turkey on Thanksgiving Day. But the situation was real, and I was able to take the knowledge that dad had shared with me and implement it.

Why was I able to do it?

I had a great coach, and I *believed* that I could. Again, my dad had not offered his opinion about how to drive. He was living proof of his knowledge of driving, which led to the belief that I, too, could do it.

If there's one thing I know you have faith in, it's the brakes on your car. Don't feel bad. So do I.

You can have the same level of faith regarding your investment skills.

Having my dad as a driving coach was invaluable. Having a coach or mentor to steer you down the road of successful investing could make all the difference in the world.

Most professionals who are tremendously talented have coaches. Tiger Woods, a tremendous golfer, still has a coach — long after he became the best golfer in the world.

And why wouldn't he?

A talented and seasoned coach can save you years of fumbling around, show you how to make tremendous progress in a fraction of the time, and help prevent major mistakes from occurring. Believe me; if I had hired a great coach twenty years ago, I'm sure it would have meant the world to me.

In biblical times, by law, the Israelites had to carry a Roman soldier's gear, or load, for a mile. Many did so begrudgingly, because they had to, and wouldn't carry it one inch further. But in Matthew 5:41, Jesus tells us, "If anyone forces you to go one mile, go with them two miles." Jesus wanted them to go the extra mile — to do more than what was required.

If you would like to have me as your coach, I'll go the second mile with you. I'll teach you about your *Decision-Maker DNA*, train you in seeing and using *The Triple Tank*, help you become a good and faithful servant, and keep you on the road to success.

Go to:

www.RonTank.com

If you love the idea of using *The Triple Tank*, but you don't feel like you have the inclination or the time to do it yourself, you may have another alternative.

Go to:

www.TheMosesFund.com

There, you will find some basic information about a new mutual fund I may be starting soon, depending on the interest I receive. Leave your e-mail address, which I promise to guard and not give to anyone else. We'll keep you updated on developments concerning *The Moses Fund* over time.

Personally, I'd rather teach you how to fish and watch you become secure in dealing with the stock market on your own, but I'm willing to help in whatever capacity I can.

By now, I'm sure you realize that my intention is not to promote the Bible as a resource to be used for making profits in the stock market. Any pastor will tell you that God did not bring about the creation of the Bible to be used as a financial guide.

At the same time, there are well over a thousand Bible verses dealing with money or personal finance — more than any other topic. One could reasonably infer that God believes it is a very important topic and one that we should understand well.

Unless we build our own cars and houses, grow our own food, and make our own clothes, we need money to acquire these things. And if we handle our money incorrectly, it could end up causing us harm.

You must keep God first, letting everything else come after Him. Keeping your relationship with God the first priority in life will keep money from establishing a stronghold in your heart that it should not have.

Money is important, but it's not more important than God.

You have an opportunity to use the *Decision-Maker DNA* and *The Triple Tank System* in the stock market to eliminate risk and become a great steward. Once you see them in action, you'll likely end up like me, wishing someone had shared them with you long ago.

I realize that making 30, 40, 50, or maybe even several 100 percent in just a few months seems hard to believe. Now that you've seen some of the proof, the believing part is up to you.

You might be thinking that this sounds too good to be true. Remember, when we first learn of God's grace, it can sound too good to be true...but it *is* true.

C. S. Lewis once said, "You can't go back and change the beginning, but you can start where you are and change the ending."

The Best Investment You'll Ever Make

*"For all long-term investors, there is only one objective –
maximum total real return after taxes."*

~Sir John Templeton

Besides the stock market, I've made investments of time, money, and energy in important parts of my life, such as education, family, church, and teaching Sunday school class. As I think about all of these life investments and how vitally important they are, I'm aware of one that is even greater.

The very best investment I have ever made was in my personal relationship with God through His son, Jesus Christ. If the only thing you take away from reading this book is excitement for making money, then I will have missed the mark because money is important, but it's not more important than God.

Throughout my life, there have been many events that have caused grief and pain. Each time, I've been able to find great comfort and peace by confiding in my heavenly Father. It comes through sitting down and talking with Him in prayer or reading and studying His written word in the Bible. This relationship with God the Father, Son, and Holy Spirit has brought joy and direction to my life, regardless of the circumstances in which

I have found myself. Knowing that God is in control, that He wants good things to come of my life, and that He is always there comforting, teaching, encouraging, and directing my steps gives me a never-ending hope.

The Bible tells me who God is, that He loves every one of us, and that His Son, Jesus, came and died on the cross to pay for all of mankind's sin. For me, that is the primary message of the Bible. It also tells me how to live, in good times and in bad, serving as an owner's manual for how I am intended to work and how to fix me when I break.

I'd like to share some verses that helped me to understand a very important message in the Bible:

Romans 6:23: "For the wages of sin is death, but the gift of God is eternal life in Christ Jesus our Lord."

Ephesians 2:8–9: "For it is by grace you have been saved, through faith—and this is not from yourselves, it is the gift of God—not by works, so that no one can boast."

John 3:16: "For God so loved the world that He gave His one and only Son, that whoever believes in Him shall not perish but have eternal life."

John 14:6: "Jesus answered, 'I am the way and the truth and the life. No one comes to the Father except through me.'"

1 Peter 2:24: "'He himself bore our sins' in his body on the cross, so that we might die to sins and live for righteousness; 'by his wounds you have been healed.'"

Luke 9:22: "And He said, 'The Son of Man must suffer many things and be rejected by the elders, the chief priests, and the teachers of the law, and He must be killed and on the third day be raised to life.'"

Romans 8:34: "Who then is the one who condemns? No one. Christ Jesus who died—more than that, who was raised to life—is at the right hand of God and is also interceding for us."

1 John 1:9: "If we confess our sins, He is faithful and just and will forgive us our sins and purify us from all unrighteousness."

Acts 2:21: "And everyone who calls on the name of the Lord will be saved."

I believe that Jesus died for my sins and sits at the right hand of my heavenly Father, interceding for me and for anyone else who calls upon His name.

I know that I'm going to heaven once this earthly life is over.

Do you?

As Sir John Templeton said, when it comes to long-term investing, there is only one objective. As people, we also need an eternal objective, a long-term maximum total return, a home in heaven.

If you are already walking with the Lord and know Him as your personal Savoir, it is my sincere hope that this book has deepened your faith and strengthened your relationship in new ways.

If you do *not* yet have a personal relationship with God, then I am inviting you, right now, to turn your life over to Jesus Christ and make heaven your future home by praying this simple prayer:

Lord Jesus,

I believe...

... that You are the Son of God.

... that You died on the cross to pay for all my sin.

... that You were buried and rose on the third day.

I confess that I am a sinner and need Your forgiveness.

Please forgive me of my sins and come into my heart.

Fill me with the Holy Spirit, and guide my life from here on.

I call upon You to be my Lord and Savior.

If you have sincerely prayed this simple prayer, then, through Christ and a new spiritual birth, you have been saved from the penalty of sin and are now a member of God's family.

Congratulations!

Now *you know* that heaven is your future home.

I encourage you to find a good Bible-based church in your area and become an active member. As a church member myself, I know just how important it is for every believer to have a healthy church home where they can connect and fellowship with other believers and grow in their faith.

I am so thankful for the opportunity to share the greatest message of all with you, and I am committed to helping people from all walks of life experience the unconditional love and unending hope found only in a personal relationship with Jesus Christ.

Please send me a note via my website, letting me know that you made the best investment ever.

www.RonTank.com

As Christians, we believe...

- ...that the entire Bible is inspired by God, without error, and is the authority on which we are to base our faith, conduct, and doctrine.

- ...in one God who exists in three distinct persons: Father, Son, and Holy Spirit. We believe that Jesus Christ is the Son of God who came to this earth as Savior of the world.

- ...that Jesus died on the cross and shed His blood for our sins. We believe that salvation is found by placing our faith in what Jesus did for us on the cross. We believe that Jesus rose from the dead and is coming again.

- ...that water baptism is a symbol of the cleansing power of the blood of Christ and a testimony to our faith in the Lord Jesus Christ.

- ...in the regular taking of communion as an act of remembering what the Lord Jesus did for us on the cross.

- ...that every believer should be in a growing relationship with Jesus by obeying God's Word, by yielding to the Holy Spirit, and by being conformed to the image of Christ.

- ...that, as children of God, we are overcomers and more than conquerors, and God intends for each one of us to experience the abundant life that He has in store for us.

Following is a prayer from my grandmother, written in the Bible she gave me, which I use today.

For whom could you do the same?

You may be surprised at the difference it can make and how long they will value it.

Dec 10/1991

To Ronald Wayne Lank Jr

Dear Grandson.

My prayer is as you read God's Word. He will reveal himself to you in a special way. and he will give you understanding of his Word, and give you Wisdom and Knowledge. and cause you to grow into the fulness in Christ Jesus. and he will always instruct and teach you in the way you should go. and Guide you with his eyes.

God Bless and keep you in his Care, I love you

Grandma

About The Author

"The highest courage is to dare to appear to be what one is."

~John Lancaster Spalding

Ron Tank

Investing The Right Way For The Right Reasons

If you want a biblically based, proven system for eliminating risk in the stock market, then you are in the right place.

Ron Tank has been called, "The Moses of Wall Street. "Known to his friends and clients simply as Tank, he coaches new and experienced investors on how to eliminate risk and maximize returns in the stock market.

As a Sunday school teacher and expert investor, Ron offers an extremely unique combination of field-proven strategy, real-life-tested biblical advice, and practical tips that successful investors need to win in today's financial markets.

Ron gained national attention and recognition when he was profiled with his brother in *Investor's Business Daily* after submitting his astounding 3,460 percent gain, turning $40,000 into over $2.2 million in eighteen months.

Through his deep study of the Bible and twenty years of hands-on investing experience, Tank has discovered timeless truths about investing that really work.

The Moses of Wall Street reveals his proven *Triple Tank System*™ which helps investors eliminate risk and maximize gains. It teaches them to profit by investing the right way for the right reasons.

Ron Tank is a devoted husband and father of two, an ordained Baptist deacon, a Sunday school teacher, and he loves being in the woods, close to God's creation. He grew up in a small town in Ohio and graduated cum laude from Ohio University with degrees in computer systems and management. He has never worked or lived near Wall Street and remains in Ohio today. This is his first book.

"And whatever you do, in word or in deed, do everything in the name of the Lord Jesus, giving thanks to God the Father through Him."

~*Colossians 3:17*

Claim Your Free Bonus Gifts!

Dear Reader,

After reading my book, I want to deepen your understanding of what I have presented to you in this book. To do that, I want to give you some great content that was created for my private coaching clients, all free.

My goal is to prove to you that I can help you become the investor you desire to be and the one God wants you to be. Ultimately, I hope you'll become a customer for life. **This can truly be a new beginning for your investing future.**

The Investor Mindset Audio Program is the first topic I share with my clients. You'll learn how I think as an investor, how my faith and the lessons I've learned from the Bible provide a rock-solid mindset for investing in the stock market.

The Special Report, *The Triple Tank Stocks Update*, will provide you with additional Triple Tank stocks occurring after the publication of this book. You'll find these stocks look very similar to the ones in the "Want Proof? The Triple Tank" chapter. They make for great models to study and learn from.

Plus, you'll also get access to three of my exclusive investor training videos that we're created for my coaching clients. With these videos, you'll feel like you are in my office, sitting at my desk and looking over my shoulder at my computer screen. But you can watch at your convenience from your own home or office.

I hope all of these resources benefit you tremendously and bring the value of the book to life. Even though the cover states these bonuses are worth $300, I firmly believe the value is far greater! It's my gift to you for investing in my book and taking action to learn more! But while money is important, it's not more important than God, so before you take your next step, pray about it first!

For details, and to accept your free gifts, visit: www.RonTank.com/BookBonus

Here's a summary of what you'll gain access to:

- **The Investor Mindset Audio Program**
  What's inside the successful investor's mind? In this audio, I'll share how I believe a successful investor must think. Plus, you'll discover how my faith and lessons I've learned from the Bible provide a rock-solid mindset for investing in the stock market. This audio was originally created just for my coaching program and is the first topic I share with my clients.

- **Special Report – The Triple Tank Stocks Update**
  This Special Report will provide you with additional Triple Tank stocks occurring after the publication of this book. You'll find these stocks look very similar to ones in the "Want Proof? The Triple Tank" chapter. They make for great models to study and learn from.

- **3 Exclusive Investor Training Videos**
  These training videos were originally created for my private coaching clients and have never been publicly shared before. With these videos, you'll feel like you are in my office, sitting at my desk and looking over my shoulder at my computer screen. But you can watch at your convenience from your own home or office.

- **And More...**

  In addition to all of the above, I have a few surprises planned to share with you that are all designed to help you learn *The Triple Tank System* for investing in the stock market. All free!

I hope you will take action and continue to invest in yourself by visiting the website below, registering your book, and claiming your gifts.

www.RonTank.com/BookBonus

Offer subject to change without notice.

Investor Training Programs

Biblical Principles for Bulletproof Investing Audios
This in-depth interview is like spending 5 hours of one-on-one time with me, at your convenience. Listen and learn the biblical principles that lead to successful investing and are the foundation for my life. I'll personally share with you what the Decision-Maker DNA and The Triple Tank System mean to me. Those hours will be well invested and bring the book to life!

The Follow the Wise Men Strategy
On Wall Street, who doesn't want to follow the wise men? Just like in biblical times, the wise men knew how to find great value. Finding and following the wise men is the easiest way to succeed! This strategy is so simple, you'll wonder why you didn't think of it!

The Triple Tank System Home Study
The Moses of Wall Street, combined with the *Triple Tank System Strategy Guide and Model Book* are a complete training system designed to provide you with the knowledge you need to use The Triple Tank strategies in the stock market. This is a proven system for minimizing your risk and maximizing your gains. PLUS, you'll have access to our exclusive "members only" online learning center filled with audios, investor training videos, resources, my personal reading list and more...

Investor Coaching Programs
For those of you who wish to go deeper and learn from me personally, I offer two live coaching programs per year. These

programs are taught by me personally. PLUS, you receive the complete home study program, and access to my online training center as described above.

I only wish someone would have offered me this training 25 years ago! The only way you'll know if I can truly help is to take the next step and invest more in yourself. Everything above comes with a 100% money-back guarantee. You have nothing to lose and everything to gain! I've eliminated all your risk!

**To purchase any of the above simply go to:
www.RonTank.com**

Therefore, as we have opportunity,
let us do good to all people,
especially to those who belong
to the family of believers.
~ Galatians 6:10

The Moses Fund™
Mutual Fund*

Knowing that many people may not have the desire or time to learn how to actively invest and manage their own money using the *Triple Tank System* system, Ron Tank is in the early stages of exploring creating a mutual fund which will invest using the same time-tested and proven methods described in this book.

If you would like more information, please go online and join our email notification list, and we will keep you updated.

If you are an accountant or attorney, or you have other skills in the mutual fund arena and are interested in becoming part of the development team, please contact us at:

www.TheMosesFund.com

*NOTE: We are not soliciting, selling, or providing any investment advice at this time; we are simply exploring the concept and the demand for the fund. This mutual fund will not simply be a faith-based fund; it will also be the only one whose primary strategy of timing has a biblical foundation. It will also be managed with biblical principles. Generosity will be a main theme by encouraging and providing a simple way for the fund holders to contribute to God's work in various places throughout the country and world.

Artist JV

More Praise for...
The Moses of Wall Street

What an amazing way to share Christ with people. It is truly unique. Just thought I'd let you know.

– Brent A. Bathurst, Jacksonville, Florida

Just an update for you Ron. I sold ABMD at 92. Bought it at 73. 26% gain, not bad.

– Brett Goldstein, New York

I have never met you personally Ron but I want you to know, this is life changing for me. This will forever change my life and the things that I will be able to do not only for me but for people who need it.

I am just now working my way into learning about how the stock market works and how to properly do short term investing as well as day trading and this book that Ron has wrote is absolutely incredible!

I can promise you this is probably the best read for the stock market that there is. It is so tied to God and the Bible that it will honestly blow you away and bring you closer to God if you choose that and I absolutely love it.

So if you really want to hear an honest and down to earth person talk and explain the market then you really don't need to look any further. Ron is probably one of the most honest people in the stock market and he is truly a great guy.

– Tony Rigsby, 26, West Virginia

The Triple Tank System is priceless! I couldn't believe anyone could put this much effort into doing it "right." This is something which I can use to educate my kids when they get older. This will be the last book or system you will ever purchase.

– **Dale,** Iowa

Ron Tank has had an enormous impact on my life and has given me tools that I have found to be invaluable to my faith, and to my family's financial success.

My first trade I gained 32.9% in about 7 weeks!

For me, this was exceptional considering I had just opened the door to the stock market and had been studying only for a few weeks.

There are several other recent winners that I can attribute to Tank's coaching and direction. He has made a believer out of me, and I hope that you will allow him the opportunity to do the same for you.

– **Cassidy Boardman,** Oklahoma

I have overcome my fears about investing and winning in the market and now I'm on my way! Ron has helped me to apply valuable principles. I am grateful for his advice on how to successfully invest in the stock market.

And my son Scott and I are learning your investing system together. Spending more time with my son happens to be one more answered prayer in my life.

– **Mike Parry,** 78, Sales Manager (Retired), Ohio

Made in the USA
Columbia, SC
04 April 2018